MY BEDROOM IS AN OFFICE
& OTHER
INTERIOR DESIGN DILEMMAS

Joanna Thornhill

Laurence King Publishing

Contents

Some people seem to be born with an innate love of interior design and an overwhelming desire to renovate and improve their home and the things in it. But others don't give the topic much consideration until they find themselves in possession of keys, walls and other such grown-up home-related things. Whichever camp you're in, it can be daunting to navigate all that Pinterest fodder and Instagram #inspo to get to the nitty-gritty.

Broken down into clear, easy-to-follow advice, with each topic tackling a real-life decorating dilemma, *My Bedroom is an Office* covers an array of challenges most homeowners (or renters) will encounter at some stage, and photographs of beautiful yet attainable spaces, taken by both professionals and keen amateurs, illustrate each point. The hands-on decorating or DIY advice is aimed at the optimistic novice keen to learn more about this daunting new realm, yet with very limited knowledge and little more in their toolkit than a few rogue screwdrivers and some leftover Allen keys from a flat-pack superstore.

With this book, as with many things in life, it makes sense to begin at the beginning, but the advice is non-sequential: keep it on your coffee table (don't worry, there's a page on how to arrange that just so to create the perfectly styled vignette), ready to reach for whenever you need a helping hand with a decorating dilemma. This book is designed to hold your hand as you navigate your way around home improvements, decorating hacks and how to create a home to be proud of – even if your office *is* a little cubbyhole at the end of your bed.

I just got the keys – now what?

In brief: Put the kettle on (if you can find it), take a deep breath and get out your notepad

Many of us suffer from Blank Space Procrastination when starting a new project (it might not be a medically recognized condition, but I'm pretty sure it's a thing), so, now the kettle's boiled, grab a pen and paper and pop on a pair of imaginary blinkers to obscure the chaos that is inevitably surrounding you right now. Walk around your new space and think how you might best live in it: if you're renting, or have spent every last penny on purchasing these four walls in the first place, chances are you won't be reaching for the sledgehammer any time soon, so – kitchen and bathroom aside – have a good tour to get an idea of which rooms make the most sense for which purpose.

If some restructuring *is* on the cards, however, try to envisage the space without walls: which rooms would you like to go where? Would it be better if the kitchen and bathroom swapped places? Would knocking through into the side return give you a sociable kitchen/dining space and allow you to squeeze in a small study at the front? Getting a builder round early on will help you to determine what's achievable, and might even get you thinking of other possibilities, even if you'll have to wait a few years before funds allow you to realize them.

Next comes the tough bit: do nothing! Well, obviously unpack the essentials, but put down those colour charts for now. Spend at least a few days, if not weeks, simply living there to see how your new home works for you. Note how the light falls in certain rooms at certain times, if there are areas you find yourself gravitating towards, if other spots feel redundant. Be aware of how you're moving around: is that door between the two reception rooms in a really annoying place, or does the position of a radiator leave you with nowhere sensible to put the TV? Jot it all down and get other family members to do the same, until a clear picture begins to form.

Now, as a reward for all that patience, you can finally start thinking about how to furnish and decorate your space. Luckily, you've got the rest of this book to help with that …

See also page 86: I'm furnishing my room from scratch – how do I work out what to put where?

It can be helpful to cover all your walls in bog-standard white paint to begin with, especially if they're in a bit of a mess, or a mishmash of garish colours. Even if you end up repainting everything, the crisp white will act as an undercoat, and let you make decisions about colour against a neutral background. If you plan to change the flooring or restore old floorboards, do it sooner rather than later.

Should I go for built-in or free-standing furniture?

In brief: Often, a combination can offer premium storage while retaining character

From ill-considered interiors in a new-build to older properties with all their quirks, most homes have a corner that's hard to furnish, owing to wonky walls, sloping ceilings or simply an awkward gap. Built-in furniture can seem quite a commitment, and it is indeed an investment in the bones of a property rather than (necessarily) something you can take away with you in the future, so it's understandably less appealing to those in more transient circumstances. Yet, while you can easily spend a small fortune on high-end bespoke joinery, it is equally simple to craft yourself a real bargain.

Built-in furniture can feel less intrusive than free-standing, particularly if fussy detail is kept to a minimum or the materials are painted the same colour as the surrounding walls. However, having too many built-in elements can take away soul, especially if it comprises mainly doors that leave little space to display signs of your personality and taste. Decide what you want to be the star of the show in your room, and work back from that. A vintage armoire might shine when paired with a slick built-in storage unit on one side; or you can strike a *wabi-sabi* balance by playing with built-ins that allow an element of customization – with a mixture of open shelving and closed cabinetry, say.

If the pennies are tight, see how much you could do yourself and get in a carpenter or tradesman for the rest. If you're at least able to work out what you want down to the small details, provide rough measurements and prepare the room before handing over to a pro, you might find the bespoke option a lot more affordable than you imagine. Choosing less luxurious materials will also help to keep the cost down, and basic pine or MDF can look just as good as hardwood if it is treated to a lick of paint at the end, or jazzed up with jewel-like handles. If in doubt, consider cheating your way to the best of both worlds by adding wooden framing around existing free-standing furniture that stretches from wall to wall or fits in an alcove, using decorator's caulk to fill any joins, to take wardrobes or bookcases visually from floor to ceiling.

Above left: It's wise to take into account elements that you wish to incorporate into a built-in space from the start: here, storage baskets fit perfectly into the shelving, which is much easier than seeking out baskets later to exactly fit a recently completed storage spot. Likewise, if building a seating nook, sourcing a shop-bought seat pad and creating the framework to incorporate it will be cheaper than having a bespoke pad made later on.

Above right: Bespoke is often the only viable option for small, tricky corners like this oddly shaped alcove, although fixing some custom-cut clothes rails directly to the walls would be a cost-effective way of achieving a similar effect on a budget.

Below: If you search long enough, you might stumble across an item of furniture that happens to (more or less) fit an alcove or area you need to furnish. Ensure you have measurements saved somewhere to hand, such as in a notebook or on your phone, so you can easily check dimensions if you find the right piece.

I'm scared of colour

In brief: Easy does it, then: dip a toe in first

Colour almost became a dirty word in interiors a decade or two ago, partly thanks to its liberal and sometimes less than flattering use in the 1980s. But it has been creeping slowly back in among the cognoscenti, leaving bland beige interiors in the shade. If you've always played it safe and aren't feeling that brave, but are still a little colour-curious, stick to your neutral backdrop and simply add bolder colours in smaller areas. It can help to start with soft furnishings and accessories that can be moved around, such as lamps and cushions, enabling you to get used to that flash of brightness in a few different places. Part-painted furniture looks fresh and contemporary: a splash of yellow on a chair leg, for example, is far less daunting than an all-over bold hue – and is easy to remedy later with a lick of neutral paint over the top.

Once you've lived with a few pieces that pop, start branching out into artworks, curtains and other larger pieces. Sticking to just a few tones will make your scheme easier on the eye, and enable you to shop with confidence, knowing that everything will hold together well. If in doubt, temper warm colours with cooler ones to stop a scheme becoming overwhelming: picture the sunny reds and yellows found on one side of the colour wheel against the more sombre blues and greens on the other. While a large, bold piece may feel like a scary step, it can actually look more cohesive and considered than numerous smaller pops of colour scattered around.

If you're still feeling brave, consider adding a little colour to the interior itself by painting a contained area of a room – perhaps an alcove wall, internal door or skirting board – in a vibrant hue, allowing it to sing. Experiment with temporary colour by trying a removable vinyl wall sticker on a key wall, or even use a strip of washi tape to create a colourful trim along the edge of a shelf. If you're still in doubt, test the colour in a lesser-used space: the downstairs loo or spare bedroom can be ideal for a bit of fun, safe in the knowledge it's not a spot you usually spend lots of time in, should you find it all a bit much.

See also page 32: Colour combining explained

Above: Tonal colour pops within an otherwise neutral space can be a fairly foolproof way of incorporating colour. Sticking to one tonal spectrum allows you to play around safely as colours within the same family should always work well together without providing any overwhelming contrasts.

Below: Grey is neutral enough to take on most other tones, so try using it as a background to more vibrant colours, like this zingy yellow and fresh mint green. Adding flashes of the same tone within tiny details, such as candlesticks and flowers, helps pull things together without overpowering the space.

Tip

Adding a few simple patterns can help the eye to move around the space more freely, and take the intensity of block colours down a notch.

How can I make my bedroom more relaxing?

In brief: Strip out the superfluous and choose calming colours and natural materials

Getting your head down for the night in a calming sanctuary needn't be restricted to those rare stays in luxury hotels. A room that enhances your well-being and aids relaxation deserves to be part of daily life, and its benefits are far more than merely aesthetic pleasure. More than any other room in the house, you want to banish all clutter here, so choose hardworking furniture that makes the most of the space (such as wardrobes that extend to the ceiling, and beds with integrated storage underneath) to minimize the opportunity for piles of stuff. Colour is an important factor in how restful the space feels, and it can be best to choose a natural palette, such as earthy greens for visual softness, blues to promote tranquillity or tones of taupe for cosiness. Rather than creating a feature wall, which would draw the eye, pick an all-round colour, even including ceilings and floors if you're feeling brave, for an enclosed, cocoon-like effect.

Bedlinen often ends up being the star of the show in the bedroom, so don't overlook this crucial element. Choose good-quality fabrics: linen or brushed cotton are wonderfully tactile, while silk – if you overlook the 1980s bachelor-pad connotations – is undeniably luxurious and also good for the skin. Sticking to plain duvet covers allows you to mix and match contrasting pillowcases, cushions and throws to change the look and make the bed inviting. Add rugs or carpet to floors, too, for extra cosiness.

Aesthetics aside, uninterrupted sleep should be the priority when you are kitting out your bedroom. Sleeping in a dark and quiet space allows the body to produce the antioxidant hormone melatonin, so help the process along by choosing thick curtains or blinds lined with blackout fabric, and go old-school by sticking to analogue alarms, keeping anything bright and bleeping strictly out of the bedroom. Incorporating natural elements can enhance the atmosphere, so sneak in foliage where you can, and choose natural materials for furniture and accent pieces wherever possible.

Above: A semi-unmade bed, featuring loose linens and a touch of the mismatched, often holds the most inviting appeal, rather than an overly prim and starched, somewhat soulless-looking spot.

Below left: A bank of wardrobes can offer an alternative to walls as a place to add a contained amount of pattern within a bedroom. A striking mural, like this delicate wooded vista, adds interest while retaining an air of calm.

Below right: Using the same colour or material on both walls and furnishings is an unusual yet effective way to minimize visual clutter in a bedroom. A headboard or fittings painted all in the same hue help blur the boundaries within the space and reduce distracting shapes and outlines.

I love the trend for houseplants, but I don't have green fingers!

In brief: Choose your plants wisely and they should do well, even with a little neglect

Not since the 1970s have houseplants enjoyed such popularity, in part fuelled by gardenless urbanites hankering for the feeling of fingers-in-soil and a connection to the outdoors. However, many lack practical know-how when it comes to our green-leaved housemates, so tough, low-maintenance specimens such as ferns, monstera and all manner of desert plants – strikingly sculptural, (reasonably) tolerant of neglect and reassuringly difficult to kill – are both a sensible and a stylish choice.

Even if you choose 'easy' plants though, it's important to get to know them: keep a note of their names, do a little research and save a list of the basic likes and dislikes of each, including their requirements for light, water and heat. It might surprise you to learn that over-watering is a far bigger culprit in houseplant-icide than being forgotten, so ensure that you check the moisture level in each pot before watering (try sticking a finger an inch or so into the soil; if it feels totally dry, the plant probably wants a drink). Make sure there's somewhere for that water to drain to: either pot the plant in a container with a drainage hole and a tray or saucer underneath, or, if you're using a solid-based pot, place a layer of gravel in the bottom to help prevent the roots from rotting. Use appropriate compost for the type of plant (succulents and cacti fare best in gritty compost, for example), and feed with a little fertilizer during the summer months, when your plants should perk up and start growing.

Tillandsia (commonly known as air plants), rather alien-looking beings that survive merely on water and air, can be a good starting point if you're a total novice, since they require little more than a weekly bath in filtered water, and can be displayed in various creative ways. The rosary vine or string of hearts (*Ceropegia woodii*), a trailing plant, is striking yet requires little care. If all else fails, try faking it with an artificial plant; there are some surprisingly convincing ones out there, and it'll be our little secret.

Above left: Making a succulent-filled 'miniature garden', like the one in the foreground, can be surprisingly satisfying. Choose your plants wisely, ensuring they suit the space and are likely to get along well together, then place some gravel in the bottom of the container (a wide-mouthed bowl will work well) before adding cactus potting mix. Arrange your plants until you are happy before fully planting, then top with moss or gravel.

Above right: Trailing plants cascading from ceiling-mounted hanging baskets can look show-stopping, but if you're nervous about fixing anything heavy to your own ceilings, simply place the plants on high shelves and allow their leaves to tumble gently downwards, or suspend from a tall item of furniture using an S-hook.

Below: Play with heights and pot styles when it comes to plant arrangements to create an artfully casual yet curated look: the foliage will work to visually tie everything together despite any mismatch in shape and design. Cheat, if necessary, by using books or *objets* to raise the odd planter and give a more varied look.

How do I bring modernity to my period property?

In brief: Carefully balance the elements that should take centre stage with what is best blended into the background

In past decades there was a trend for the 'modernization' of old housing stock, and many beautiful period features were ripped from buildings in favour of a more contemporary finish. Thankfully, we now know better, on the whole, and treat the bones of our homes with more respect, appreciating the details and quirks unique to older properties. That doesn't mean that living in a heritage home should entail sticking slavishly to decorating according to its era, however. Period features can offer a surprisingly neutral backdrop for various modern styles, and juxtaposing a panelled wall or picture rail with a contemporary colour scheme or design-led pieces can create a soulful, balanced living space. There are various ways to avoid your home feeling like a museum, and to retain functionality while preserving character.

Broadly, there are two approaches: blend it in or let it sing. Taking the subtle route can still be bold and striking, for example painting the wall around an original cast-iron fireplace in a similar dark tone, giving it a gently moody, contemporary feel and allowing the eye to discover the feature as it moves over it, rather than shouting for attention. The latter approach, on the other hand, can be a great way to highlight standout features, such as framing show-stopping cornicing with a contrasting paint colour and choosing clean-lined, simple, modern furnishings that allow the period element to take centre stage in an otherwise fuss-free room.

You could also try a more offbeat way to give period spaces a modern twist. If a wall is missing its original dado rail, for example, nod to the room's past by running a strip of copper tape horizontally across the wall at a similar height, or simply paint the lower part of the walls a different colour, with just a neat join between. Act deliberately, perhaps contrasting a futuristic light fitting with ornate cornicing or mixing a 1950s sideboard with a brand-new armchair against Victorian-inspired wallpaper. And don't overlook the details: a contemporary light switch, door handle or radiator can provide the balance to create a look that's considered, rather than dated.

Many traditional wallpaper manufacturers now offer reworked versions of archive classics, simplifying the original designs or respectfully refreshing them in new colourways. Using such a design can strike just the right contemporary tone in a period property, especially when treated in unexpected ways, like mixing two different colourways together within the same space.

BEGINNER'S TOOLKIT: Essential DIY staples for any household

There comes a time in adulthood when the prospect of investing in a decent, comprehensive set of tools, rather than making do with the few scrappy bits you've accumulated so far, seems eminently sensible. But if you're not sure what to invest your earnings in, here are some basic starter pieces.

1. Tools
• Screwdriver: A full set of heads in varying sizes, suitable for straight, cross-head and Pozidriv screws, is ideal, although a ratchet multi-head screwdriver can be invaluable as well. Look for heads with magnetic tips, for minimal dropped-screw frustration.
• Cordless power drill: It's worth spending a little more on a decent model, since you'll use it more than you expect. Choose a combination model with hammer, rotary drilling and screwdriver modes, to get the most bang for your buck.
• Hacksaw: Don't let its diminutive size fool you; the humble hacksaw can make light work of plastic, metal and smaller pieces of wood, and its blades are interchangeable.
• Hammer: Choose one with a claw head for wrenching out nails. Buy a chunky model with some weight, rather than anything flimsy.
• Pliers: Useful for anything that needs gripping, bending or cutting. Fine-nose pliers can be useful for fiddly jobs; pump pliers are the hardworking wrench-types; and cutting pliers, well, cut things.

2. Painting and Decorating
• Set of paintbrushes: Don't fall for the false economy of purchasing cheap ones; you'll just spend half your time picking rogue bristles from your paintwork. Buy several different widths: say, a 25mm for cutting in, 50mm for wood trim, 75mm for doors and 100mm or wider for walls and ceilings.
• Paint tray and roller: A medium-pile roller is the best all-rounder, while a foam roller will give the best finish if you are applying oil-based paint or varnish to furniture. Make life easier

if you're painting several different colours at the same time and line each tray with an old carrier bag, for speedy clean-ups.

• Sandpaper: A multipack of different grades should see you through most basic tasks. A low grit (40–60) is good for heavy sanding or stripping; 80–120 is the all-rounder for everyday surface smoothing; while a finer grit of 360+ is useful for finishing surfaces, such as in furniture restoration.

• Filler: Your go-to for filling small holes and rectifying minor imperfections in plasterwork. Polyfilla is easy to grab for small, quick jobs, especially if you buy the pre-mixed type, while decorator's caulk works well for providing a neat finish along gaps between walls and woodwork.

• Glue: Hot glue guns are inexpensive and have many crafty uses. It's worth keeping an epoxy resin adhesive and wood glue in your kit as well, to cover all eventualities.

3. Odds and Sods

• Tape measure: Don't buy anything under 3m long. Look for retractable metal ones with both metric and imperial measurements, and a decent locking button.

• Torch: The notion of sitting around by candlelight during a power cut might be romantic, but practical it's not. When buying a torch, look out for the 'lumens' (light capacity). FL-1 generally indicates that it's a good model, while the higher the lumens per watt, the brighter it'll be.

• Spirit level: No, you can't just use the app on your phone! Go for a decent-sized, bona fide spirit level with both horizontal and vertical levels. If you're feeling fancy, choose one with a magnetic base, a rotating vial or even a laser.

• Utility knife: Those with rubber-coated handles are the comfiest to hold, and buying one with built-in storage for spare blades will prevent you from scrabbling frantically for replacements when one snaps or blunts.

• Toolbox: Well, you've got to keep it all somewhere. Choose one with several compartments for keeping all your hardware in order, along with removable trays and bins for tools. If you're amassing quite a bit of kit, a stackable rolling toolbox offers portability and tons of storage.

3

Should I go open-plan?

In brief: Think carefully about how you would use the opened-up space, and if it would work for you both now and in five years' time

Large, airy open spaces are undoubtedly more in vogue these days than warrens of tiny, dark, disjointed rooms. Yet racing to knock down every internal wall in sight can lead to regret if you then realize you have no way of escaping the piles of washing-up/sofa-eating dog/acres of ugly plastic kids' toys. In fact, in recent years there has even been a shift back towards separate living spaces.

Of course, open-plan living *can* work wonderfully in the right environment, providing an area large enough for several family members to carry out various different tasks while still being together in one place. Designers often talk about 'flow', and the wall-free home can allow free and unrestricted movement. But for most people, a modicum of flexibility and defined separation is still the best option. The classic two-reception terraced house is often opened up to create a more generous living area, which is undeniably more versatile and sociable, but consider installing sliding doors or a floor-length curtain to enable you to turn your sitting room back into a cosy, intimate den when required. Take an educated guess at what the future might hold: an open-plan space with young children will allow you to keep a closer eye on them, but when your angelic cherubs transform into sulky teens, will you still want to be spending all your time with them?

There are ways to get the best of both worlds. A dining space incorporated into a larger kitchen/dining area will certainly get more use than a shut-off dining room, so consider consolidating these areas while retaining a separate living room. Alternatively, retain an element of boundary by creating a large opening between two spaces, rather than removing all walls completely. Let your home's footprint guide you: for example, an L-shaped space lends itself naturally to creating a nook for a cooking or dining area that has a degree of separation while remaining part of the overall space.

See also page 118: I have no entryway

Above: Bold pops of bright colour within this space, with the same flooring running throughout, help the two areas feel united, but each has its own identity. The partially retained dividing wall clearly delineates the space's two functions: dining and lounging. Painting the dining area a darker colour helps to zone the space further, yet the dark hue ties in with the hearth in the living area.

Below left: The half-height wall partially obscuring the kitchen creates a space sociable enough to interact with others in different areas, while clearly defining the cooking area from the rest of the room. A spot like this would work well as a breakfast bar, with space to tuck a few high stools beneath it on the 'living' side of the room, offering a defined eating area despite the very limited footprint.

Below right: Placing a dining area between the kitchen and living spaces in an open-plan flat offers a degree of separation between the areas for cooking and for relaxing, despite being in close proximity. The painted triangle on the wall behind the dining table cleverly marks its position, reinforcing the visual separation of the spaces.

Are there limits to where I can use wallpaper?

In brief: Yes … but its use is probably broader than you think

In recent years wallpaper has returned with a bang, and as our familiarity and confidence with it grow, so too does our desire to use it in bolder and more experimental ways. Not only is it increasingly being used all over, rather than just on feature walls, but it is also cropping up in less obvious areas, such as kitchens and bathrooms. Instantly softening their somewhat sterile nature (and sometimes cheaper per metre than tiles), wallpapering these spaces gives a wow factor and focal point to a room where pattern is otherwise limited.

Of course, since most are paper-based, placing wallpaper somewhere it will be in direct contact with water is a no-no, but by following a few basic rules you can broaden its use greatly. How to treat wallpaper depends on where it is placed: you can hang it directly behind a sink, bath or hob, but fit clear acrylic panelling or toughened glass over the top and ensure it is well sealed to protect it. Or stick to tiles or splashbacks in wet spots, and save wallpaper for less hardworking areas, such as walls away from cooking or washing facilities, or even the ceiling, for an unexpected hit of bold pattern. For extra durability, apply a protective layer of decorator's varnish over the top of the wallpaper, but practise on a spare scrap first to ensure that you're happy with the finish. Consider the type of wallpaper, too: the plastic coating on vinyl wallpaper makes it durable, but a non-woven paper can be a better choice for humid rooms, allowing the walls to breathe.

If you're still too daunted to put wallpaper on actual walls, try placing it on furniture instead: pick out details such as drawer fronts, use it to line the back of a bookcase or cupboard, or completely cover an item to create a striking centrepiece. Make sure that the surface of the furniture is clean and flake-free before you begin, using sandpaper to remedy any lumps and bumps. Use wallpaper paste to attach the paper, or, if you're after a quick fix on a smaller area, cheat with double-sided tape. For a neat finish, cut the paper roughly to size before sticking it down, then use a sharp craft knife to slice off any excess.

See also page 100: Is the feature wall a cliché?

Above left: This striking wallpaper, featuring Fornasetti's famous 'theme and variation' plate series, works wonderfully as an unexpected, show-stopping design accent in an otherwise neutral bathroom space, cleverly drawing the eye upwards. Despite the bold design, it doesn't overwhelm, thanks to the restrained colour and simplicity of the rest of the room.

Above right: Although it has a strong geometric pattern, the pared-back palette of this pastel-hued wallpaper almost acts as a neutral backdrop for the vibrant painted dining chairs and candlesticks. Alongside the bold chequerboard floor, it adds warmth and interest without taking centre stage.

Below: Situated away from ovens, hobs and sinks, wallpaper can generally be used freely. Even if it's not close to washing or cooking facilities, do bear in mind the room's size and extraction system: wallpaper in a small space with poor ventilation or high humidity may be more susceptible to light damage over time than in a larger area.

I have no space for a bedside table

In brief: Then use something else, or use your walls rather than the floor

Having the room for full bedside tables flanking your bed is often more of a luxury than a given, particularly if you have under-bed drawers. But whatever space you have, there's probably a way of creating a spot for your morning cuppa and favourite novel. The obvious starting point is to look for furniture that you could use instead. A slim stool takes up a fraction of the space of a bedside table and provides just enough surface area to house the basics; you can even make the most of the space underneath it with a stack of books or a pretty yet practical storage basket. The steps of a wooden ladder leaning against the wall can provide 'shelf space' to rest a few books on, or to drape ties or jewellery over.

The walls, however, may prove to be your best friend. Installing simple shelving (or even a small wall-mounted cabinet) by your bed keeps the floor clear, and can be placed at a suitable height for reaching over to switch off your alarm clock in the morning. If space to the side is really limited, you could even mount a shelf above your bed (it might feel less precarious if you place it above the headboard and pull your bed slightly away from the wall, rather than having the shelf suspended directly above your head as you sleep). If your DIY skills are up to it, adding sides can give a neater, bespoke feel.

Lighting is, of course, crucial in a bedroom, and no one wants to have to traipse across the room to turn off the main light just before dozing off. If you can involve an electrician, then wall-mounted angled lights will free up the floor, or you could even install a suspended cable pendant either side of the bed, operated by a switch within easy reach or an on/off toggle on a switched bulb holder. If it needs to be more of a DIY affair, however, cheat your way to a similar look by hanging a plug-in pendant lamp with an attractive flex from a hook or bracket, or choose a clip-on plug-in light. Alternatively, consider a floor-standing lamp: models with a thin base could easily be tucked half underneath the bed, providing a practical yet chic solution.

Pulling your bed away from the wall even a tiny amount can open up just enough floor space to stash a few bedside essentials, without causing the bed to eat into the remaining available floor space too much. A nearby window ledge could also be used.

Tip

For a more rustic look, a basic garden tree stump could offer a charming twist (just check for insects before you haul it in, to avoid introducing any unexpected roommates into your boudoir).

I painted my place white, but it feels cold. What went wrong?

In brief: For a non-colour, white can be complicated. Choose 'dirty' whites with off-white undertones to add interest and depth

Whether it's to lighten a naturally dark space or to give a quick update to a new home, many of us use a refreshing coat of brilliant white emulsion to brighten up interior walls. However, while white is arguably the ultimate blank canvas for any space, that doesn't mean it isn't sometimes the 'wrong' choice. Pure white is unforgiving in certain scenarios, and its artificial starkness can be uncompromising and impersonal.

First, take into account the pivotal role that natural light can play, both in your specific room and in your corner of the globe more generally. The natural light in colder countries is, unsurprisingly, cooler, and can feel uncomfortably stark if the interiors don't take that into account, whereas more tropical regions receive much stronger, warmer light, enhancing the richness of bright tones. This is where selecting the right undertones comes into play. A yellow undertone, for example, will give a hint of creamy warmth, while bluer undertones look crisper. In the northern hemisphere, a south-facing living room would benefit from white with a blue/grey pigment to balance out any glare from dominant direct sunlight, while a north-facing living room will receive diffused, cooler light and therefore be better suited to a slightly sandier off-white. The reverse is true of the southern hemisphere.

Subtly mixing different tones for depth and variation – from ceilings to woodwork – helps to add a barely-there yet crucial layered feeling, while sticking to the same general undertone family within a scheme will ensure that everything hangs together well. Take into account other colours in the room that your whites might pick up, and experiment with different paint finishes. If your furnishings are mostly in earthy shades, warm whites will complement them best, while blue-hued off-whites work best against brighter, bolder tones. It's important to consider indoor lighting, too: you may need to compensate if you have unforgiving fluorescent lighting or cool white halogens, and use warmer hues; gently layered warm white lighting, on the other hand, is more forgiving.

See also page 98: I've chosen a neutral scheme – how can I jazz it up without resorting to colour?

Above: Natural materials - from the rustic wood tabletop to the fur throw and woven sisal floor rug - help prevent this otherwise neutral space from feeling stark, despite the use of white tones on both walls and floors.

Below left: Even quite simple vintage furniture can add soul and character to a space. By incorporating only warm woods and materials where colour is used, as well as utilizing lots of rounded shapes over sharp linear outlines, the look here is cosy and relaxed.

Below right: Tying together the wood tones of the exposed staircase and the furniture offers a cohesive look that still retains visual warmth when curated from honey-toned timbers like these.

Tip

If you've already pure-whited everything before reading this book, don't feel you have to repaint it all. Consider adding a couple of off-white hues to important areas only.

How can I make pieces in different styles and from different eras cohere?

In brief: Embrace the eclectic look, but make it work by ensuring that a 'common thread' holds it all together

For most of us, a home that contains a mixture of pieces is the result of circumstance rather than design, as we acquire new (or new-to-us) pieces in various ways during the course of our lives. And while trends are a great way to experiment and be inspired, following them slavishly can result in rooms that feel disingenuous and are liable to look dated very quickly. Mixing objects from different eras creates an interesting, multilayered interior that can grow organically over time, but there are a few tricks to ensuring that it appears charmingly eclectic rather than simply a jumble of hand-me-downs.

The idea of a common thread – an element that is present throughout to create unity, even if a space contains mismatched pieces – is useful. There need be only one unifying element to pull a space together visually: it could be colour – sticking to a similar scheme throughout, or using one bold accent tone for each key element – or even furnishings that are of a similar tone despite being different in design. Houseplants can provide such unity, if they feature throughout the space, or use furniture in similar styles – all with Victorian-inspired turned-wood legs, say – even if they are not part of the same range.

The bones of the room itself can provide the continuity to unite the otherwise differing elements. For example, using the same smart floorboards throughout an open-plan space, and using the same pendant light repeatedly, can help mismatched furnishings feel more deliberate (even if they're not). Aim to ensure, however, that there is a dominant bias within the space. For example, if you have a mixture of traditional, Mid-Century and contemporary pieces, try to have most in just one of those styles, rather than an equal mix of all three, allowing the rest to shine out as accents. Keep an eye on scale, too: if you are using mismatched chairs around a dining table, stick to similar shapes and heights for a more cohesive feel.

See also page 52: What can I do to avoid faddy decor?

This living space appears eclectic and bohemian, but a closer look reveals clues to careful curation that belie its casual aesthetic. Patterns, where used, have a similar style and colour palette and the bulk of the space is in predominantly neutral shades, with reds, blues and a tiny hit of yellow used to accent. While clearly compiled by someone with a great eye for design, bearing these rules in mind will help amateurs and first-timers to achieve a similar layered look.

Am I stuck with my existing wall tiles?

In brief: You might be stuck with them, but that doesn't mean you can't transform them

Many people think of tiles as a deal-breaker if they're not keen on what they've got, and it can feel as though they must be either replaced or tolerated. But there's actually a myriad grey areas between those two options. Possibly the most familiar – tile paint – often has cheap connotations (think crudely updated pub loo or budget rental flat), but if it is done well, it can look surprisingly slick. For a great finish, make sure the tiles are immaculately clean and bone dry (fungicidal wash, limescale remover and even a light sanding with fine-grade sandpaper can all be beneficial, especially if the tiles are particularly stained or very shiny), and apply the paint with a foam roller to avoid brush marks. Most specialist tile paints offer an all-in-one formula, but if you want a colour that's not available in this form, standard emulsion paint will work if you combine it with an appropriate primer and waterproof topcoat. Finish with a grout pen to complete the illusion.

Tile stickers have the reputation of being gimmicky, but these days there's a surprisingly on-trend selection available. If the area you need to cover is small, go bold and add the stickers to every tile, but for larger areas, where the cost might become prohibitive, display them in a striking strip or use them on random tiles only. This last option is also great for covering up a scheme consisting of mainly plain tiles with the odd dodgy patterned one. If your tiles are plain but feel bland, sprucing them up with a coloured grout could produce a striking transformation; grout is now available in a range of colours, from pastels to metallics. Use a grout-removing tool to get rid of old, flaky grout, then add your new colour.

If you're still not convinced, consider putting new tiles over existing ones, but bear in mind that this will work only if the original tiles are clean and sound. The old tiles can actually act as a base, and this approach certainly involves less preparation than stripping the tiles off and starting from scratch.

Above left: If your existing tiles are fine but dull (an all-over bog-standard white square, for instance), a statement sticker can double up as artwork of sorts, adding design detail to an area where actual artwork wouldn't be appropriate.

Above right: Using tile paint across an entire swathe of tiles can make it more durable than simply adding it to certain tiles, where the paint edges may be more susceptible to wear and tear. A satin or gloss finish might be the norm, but a contemporary matt paint can give a slicker look.

Below: Stone-effect stickers can be a clever way of adding a little luxe to an otherwise basic space, while allowing you to play around with on-trend materials, such as terrazzo effects.

COLOUR COMBINING EXPLAINED:
Working with tonal, harmonizing and contrasting hues

You'll doubtless have seen a colour wheel before (even if it was back in school), but it might not be something you automatically refer to when decorating. You may even remember the principles (12 hues split throughout the wheel, half cool and half warm), and how it comprises the primary colours (red, yellow and blue) flanked by the secondary (green, orange and purple) and tertiary colours (those created by mixing primaries and secondaries, such as mauve or turquoise). But it's all well and good knowing the theory; what does it mean in practice?

1. Tonal
Most colour cards consist of five or six light to dark tints and shades of the same colour, and this is exactly the same as the individual increments of the colour wheel. Tonal colours are essentially the same base colour mixed with varying amounts of white or black to alter the tonal value, producing stronger and subtler variations of that tone. Since no additional colours are involved (neither white nor black is classed as a colour), a fail-safe decorating method is simply to choose a single tone and play with these values to create a delicately layered interior. The resulting lack of drama can create a restful atmosphere that is particularly suited to spaces such as bedrooms.

2. Harmonizing
If you want to add depth and interest but not push the boat out, look at any three colours that sit side by side on the colour wheel, such as blue-green, green and yellow-green. Playing with these three colours will create a scheme that is easy on the eye while giving you greater scope for experimentation. You can still be creative with different tones, too, by working up and down that particular section of the colour wheel, for instance pairing a light aquamarine with a muddy, deep pine. Sticking with three colours on either the cool or the warm side of the colour wheel will produce a softer look, or, for something a little punchier, 'cross the boundary' and work with, for example, orange, yellow and yellow-green.

3. Contrasting

If you're keen on drama, choosing colours from opposite sides of the colour wheel will ensure that you're using contrasting but not clashing colours. This adds intrigue to any space, and how far you push it is up to you. Take red and green, for example: these are opposites that *do* attract, despite the myth attesting to the contrary. But decorating a space entirely in equal measures of fire-engine red and forest green is understandably not everyone's cup of tea, so make it work by looking once more at the tonal variations of these contrasting colours – choosing a softer sage and pairing it with a calming coral, for example – or playing with percentages, using one colour as the main event and the other as an accent.

3

How do I choose art to match my interior?

In brief: Don't (it's a bit naff) ... although you can do it the other way round, by following a few rules

A sure-fire way of upsetting an artist is to tell them that you're looking for a painting to complement your curtains. It's a fair niggle; most artists favour creative integrity over work that sits nicely next to some scatter cushions. But while the idea of choosing art purely on its own merit and not worrying about how it relates to your room is a worthy one, many of us are looking for a happy medium.

If you're redecorating a room, take any planned artwork into consideration right at the beginning, and let it inspire your design scheme via one particular element – colour, pattern or style, say – without being too literal and ending up with a matchy-matchy space. This could involve picking up on abstract shapes in the artwork and bringing elements of them into a few accessories, or adding a black-and-white photo print to a mainly monochrome interior palette. For colourful works, seek out a hue that features sparingly in the painting, and use it as an accent in the setting.

Of course, we don't always approach our interior designing this way round – particularly in organic spaces that haven't had an initial masterplan and have simply evolved – so you may find yourself seeking artwork to dress an already decorated space. You can of course reverse the advice above, but do still try to let your taste in art be your guide, rather than looking for something that matches your rug. You can always tweak the odd interior accessory afterwards to help it all hang together more cohesively.

Above: Some schemes can be so well curated, it's hard to tell whether the art or the accessories came first. By sticking to a restricted palette and mimicking shapes featured in wall art within furniture outlines and cushion patterns, the interior is united with the art to perfection.

Below left: A single statement, supersized artwork can form the backbone of the space it sits in. The delicate colour palette of this interior space allows the artwork to take centre stage, while the room itself plays a more supportive role.

Below right: Black-and-white prints or photographs can look stark in a purely monochrome space, so by mixing in some textures, plants and off-white elements, the minimalist palette is retained without things feeling soulless.

My bedroom is an office

In brief: Confine the office equipment to a specific part of the room, and create a set-up that you can easily conceal – literally or via clever design – at the end of the working day

No one wants to stare at a messy workspace at the best of times, least of all when dozing off in bed at the end of the day. But if the bedroom is your only viable space to set up shop, however small the available area, if you're savvy and organized you can create a spot that functions as a place of productivity without causing nightmares.

For the workspace itself, think about repurposing a piece of furniture that will fit the aesthetic of your bedroom. A bureau or secretaire can work brilliantly, and you can just shut the hatch when you're not using it. A simple writing desk, console or even small dining table can be a good option, but try to make a raised platform for your monitor (perhaps just a shelf resting on two wooden battens) to ensure that it sits at the correct eye level; you can tuck your keyboard under this when it's not being used. If your table has no drawers, a basic fabric skirt fixed around the top can hide a multitude of sins, from printers to power cables.

Since space will no doubt be limited, think laterally to make the most of your work nook. If your desk is in an alcove, this can offer the ideal spot to add shelves for storage, but otherwise a ladder-style leaning desk unit may be most efficient, or even a modular shelving system incorporating a desk. Soften the appearance of work paraphernalia such as box files or ring binders by covering them with fabric or wallpaper swatches that tie in with your room decor, and be creative with storage – why not keep archived paperwork in a small vintage suitcase, for example, or stack your printer paper in an old wooden fruit crate?

An ugly office chair will never enhance any bedroom, so consider working from a more visually pleasing dining chair or even a padded stool. If this is your full-time workspace, however, a proper computer chair is best for your body, so shop around for an aesthetically pleasing one (they may be few and far between, but they're out there). If you've already got a bog-standard one, try covering it with a chunky throw when it's not in use, or make fitted covers in a charming fabric to give it a more homely feel.

See also page 12: How can I make my bedroom more relaxing?

Above left: Hiding in plain sight can be a good approach for the bedroom office. Through the use of cute accessories, charming vintage furniture and a pretty overall aesthetic, this study spot is a chic addition rather than an unfortunate eyesore.

Above right: An ingenious fold-down wall desk can work wonderfully in a tiny space. A purpose-built unit allows you to keep your laptop and a few other essentials hidden away, while a wall-mounted drop-leaf table or a drop-leaf butterfly table would do a similar job.

Below: Natural materials can offer the perfect counterbalance to a tech-filled study space. Paired with simple floral cuttings and touches of greenery, this work nook looks the opposite of corporate. Clever, subtle tech, such as the lamp that incorporates a wireless charging base, allows the desktop to remain relatively cable-free.

Tip

If you're up for a DIY challenge, try converting a cupboard or wardrobe into a bijou office. Add a deep shelf across the whole space at desk height, place additional shelving above for storage, tuck your printer underneath and simply shut the door when you're done.

My windows are overlooked – how can I create more privacy?

In brief: If net curtains aren't your thing, try clever blinds, frosting films and plant-based disguises

A common problem in our urban environments is a lack of privacy. No one wants to spend the day sitting in the dark with the curtains drawn, though, so creative thinking is required if you are to enjoy some solitude indoors. Semi-sheer blinds can block prying eyes and diffuse the light, but the loss of view or context can feel a little oppressive. Bottom-up blinds – which, as the name suggests, operate the reverse way to standard roller blinds – allow you to control exactly what you can and can't see, and can be a great option where privacy needs can change throughout the day. Shutters are also wonderful for customizing levels of light and privacy, but they can be costly. A simple cafe-style curtain covering the lower half of a window is a quick, effective fix, and can be made using little more than some fabric, a line and some clips, if sewing's not your thing.

Another unsung hero, window frosting film, has experienced a boost in popularity lately. As designers begin collaborating with manufacturers, it becomes easier to find interesting, on-trend patterns on these films, which can turn your windows into a real statement. They replicate the look of acid-etched or sandblasted glass, but it is relatively straightforward to install them: just look for static-cling types, then follow the manufacturer's instructions.

Plants can also offer screening in such circumstances. A strategic hedge or tall grassy plants outside can create a barrier, or, in a flat, consider planting in window boxes. Train vines up a trellis or window grille, or hang trailing plants in front of the window, allowing their foliage to offer a delicate filter. Finally, consider the arrangement of your furniture. Sometimes, something as simple as moving a sofa, table or bed can have a big impact if it brings your point of view back into the room and away from the windows.

Despite the old-lady connotations, vintage lace can look charming (and even contemporary, in the right setting) as a window treatment. Old embroidered linens and laces can offer a delicately patterned, semi-sheer look that works well if left to hang fuss-free from a curtain wire or pole. They can also act as a clever disguise for windows with unappealing patterned glass.

Is grey the new magnolia?

In brief: Gosh, we sincerely hope so

Magnolia, once the go-to neutral tone for interior walls, has fallen out of favour in recent years, partly a victim of its own success, partly sullied by its prolific use in cheap-and-cheerful rentals. Grey has quietly been foisting it out of the way to take over the number one spot – and it is successful for good reason. With more than 50 tones and shades, it offers a nuanced backdrop that allows light to play off it in interesting ways that are impossible to achieve with mere beige.

Grey's almost chameleon-like qualities allow it to act as a neutral base for a range of different interiors styles and schemes, flattering pretty much any colour it is paired with and allowing more vibrant hues to take centre stage. Finding the right 'temperature' of grey is key to its success, however. Take into account the room's natural light (cool light usually warrants a warmer grey, and vice versa), other furnishings and decorative elements, as well as the overall style and ambience you want to achieve. Cooler blue-grey tones ooze sophistication and work well with slick Scandi schemes (think monochromatic with pops of colour), particularly suiting airy, light-filled apartments. For naturally darker, smaller or period spaces, a grey with a warm undertone of yellow or orange – or even 'greige' (yes, a mixture of grey and beige) – can be more sympathetic. This sits particularly well with the warm metallic accents that are currently on trend, and with natural wood.

Mixing a few different tones of grey in a single space can be effective, helping to enhance the contrasts between architectural details. A high, sloping ceiling might benefit from being highlighted with a darker hue, while teaming grey walls with creamy woodwork can enhance those grey tones. Try playing with paint finish, too, although – for walls, at least – grey is best in a flat matt, to avoid a metallic appearance.

See also page 26: I painted my place white, but it feels cold. What went wrong?

Above: When things are kept clean and slick, grey can add a boutique hotel vibe to a space. Mixing different tones together will add interest, and with grey-on-grey pairings, you can't really go wrong. Be sure to include white and black within your spectrum of greys, for added depth.

Below left: Arguably, grey is better associated with industrial-style spaces over luxe ones, and although it can work equally well in both, it does make a natural companion to industrial materials such as metal and concrete.

Below right: Especially at the darker end of its spectrum, grey can be used to add drama to a space, transforming alcoves and eaves into striking architectural features. Use a mix of hues to highlight such features, by making them a lighter or darker tone than the rest of the space.

My walls are too hard/soft/crumbly to put shelves on

In brief: Check your equipment to see if there's a way, or work around it

Putting up shelves is usually considered a basic DIY job: make hole in wall, fill it with Rawlplug, screw bracket on – and you're done. Not all walls are created equal, however, and some make the job much harder. It's important to establish how your walls are constructed: are they plasterboard or solid brick? Load-bearing or partition? Often a simple tap on the wall is the best way to tell. A hollow sound probably indicates plasterboard or a cavity; keep tapping around to see if you can find support battens (the sound will deaden at that point), and ensure that you put your fixings there. If the sound is consistent wherever tapped, it's likely masonry, meaning a stronger construction (this may require extra clout for drilling into). Then think about what exactly you're planning to use the shelves for – a few paperbacks and a couple of ornaments, or a hefty collection of hardbacks?

You'll need a power drill with a hammer action to make the holes (although it's advisable not to switch it to hammer mode until you've drilled through any plaster, since that might cause it to crack, especially if the wall is less than stable). The right supports are also essential: if you are working with plasterboard, you will need Redi-drivers or snap toggles to support the screws for shelves; masonry walls will simply require a Rawlplug to support the weight you estimate the shelf will take. Be generous with brackets and screw lengths (as a rule, the larger the screws and plugs, the more weight they should be able to hold).

You could also consider using adjustable shelving. The String system is chic and eminently customizable, offering a modern alternative to bog-standard slot shelving sets. The humble pegboard can work particularly well in a craft room or kitchen; some chunkier designs have the option of adding slim shelves, with the 'pegs' acting as brackets. If all else fails, there's always free-standing shelving, but do think outside the box: could you create a shelving system by fixing slim ledges to a sheet of sturdy wood and simply leaning it against the wall, or install some shelving within a wooden 'frame' that fits in a corner but looks more built-in than a bookcase?

See also page 8: Should I go for built-in or free-standing furniture?

A picture ledge or a wall-mounted magazine rack allows you to display books or magazines front-facing while leaving them accessible. You could even nestle in the odd art print or small decorative *objet* among them too, should the mood take you.

Tip

Remedy an oversized screw hole by sticking a (de-headed) matchstick into the gap, to tighten things up.

Can I modernize my old furniture?

In brief: It's worth doing your homework first, but generally – yes!

Some of us are born with vintage furniture, some go out and buy vintage, and some have vintage thrust upon us. Whatever your circumstances, probably not all of it will be to your exact taste, but doing something potentially irreversible to an old or heirloom piece is understandably daunting.

If you're concerned about desecrating something of genuine historical merit, perform a few basic checks before brandishing the sandpaper. There is no definitive cut-off date for an object to be classified as antique, but generally anything older than 50 years could be considered as such. Look for signs of good craftsmanship – dovetail joints, decorative details that aren't perfectly uniform or symmetrical (hinting that the piece has been hand- rather than machine-made), no cracks – and note the materials themselves; if it's solid hardwood rather than veneer, for example, or if upholstery is stuffed rather than sprung. Next, look at the condition. Superficial scratches or a wobbly leg might be easily remedied, but if there are signs of rot or damp, renovating might be difficult and turn out not to be worth the time or money.

If your item turns out to be a lower-value mass-produced retro piece, or has value-degrading damage, yet is still functionally sound, don't be afraid to go ahead and refinish, customize or upcycle it. In fact, discovering that a piece has little inherent worth can sometimes be a good thing, since it gives you carte blanche to do what you want free of guilt or worry. Refurbishing something rather than throwing it into landfill and buying a replacement is always better for the environment, not to mention your budget, and it may ease your conscience if you opt to spruce up something that's already suffering from wear and tear, rather than renovate an item that is in pristine condition but not to your taste. The pages overleaf detail various ways to paint furniture. With older pieces, do be sympathetic to the original materials and allow them to breathe, by treating them with natural wax colours or finishes rather than artificial stains and varnishes.

See also page 22: Are there limits to where I can use wallpaper?

An old chair enjoys a thoroughly modern overhaul in a glorious clash of colour and pattern, with a new coat of glossy pink paint and re-upholstery in African fabrics. An accent piece like this can let you go to town far more than you might on a prominent, everyday item, and it's easy enough to repaint or re-cover if you end up finding it a bit much later on.

PAINTING FURNITURE: What to use and where to use it

Customizing furniture with paint is an economical, enjoyable way to create a piece that fits in perfectly with the rest of your decor, without hitting the shops. Here are five ideas anyone can try.

1. Gloss paint has fallen somewhat out of fashion in recent years, but a vibrant, glossy coat can give a pleasing contemporary twist to a piece of vintage furniture. Its hardwearing finish makes it a good choice for pieces situated in high-traffic areas such as hallways or children's rooms.

2. Cheat your way to well-worn chic while avoiding the shabby by creating a distressed effect. Apply a water-based wood stain to an unpainted or unvarnished piece of wooden furniture (or remove old paint/varnish with sandpaper first), then, when it is dry, apply matt emulsion paint roughly over the top, leaving some parts of the wood uncovered. Allow to dry, then rub over the whole piece with a sanding block, applying varying pressure at random, before sealing with a coat of clear furniture wax.

3. For a two-tone distressed finish, so that the piece appears as if its topcoat has chipped off over time to reveal a former paint colour from a past life, paint on your casually-peeking-through colour first. Apply petroleum jelly or wax to the corners and edges where you want the base colour to show through, then paint the second contrasting colour on top. Rub the corners and edges with sandpaper to remove the top layer of paint and reveal the colour underneath.

4. Chalk paint is often associated with delicate, natural tones and grand armoires in seventeenth-century French chateaux, but there's no reason not to give a traditional piece of dark wood furniture a contemporary twist with a bolder hue for a look that works in a more modest setting. Here, carved details are picked out with a blue accent, and the piece has received minimal ageing effects, so that it remains modern yet with a nod to history. Get the look by rubbing the accent paint on with an almost-dry brush or cloth after the main piece is painted.

5. Simple paint effects are strikingly effective and can be achieved with little more than masking tape. Paint the whole piece in the base colour of your choice, leave to dry, then apply masking tape in a pattern. To prevent the paint from bleeding, paint back over the taped lines with the base colour and leave to dry before adding the contrasting colour in the gaps. Peel off the tape, fix any slip-ups with a small artist's brush, and marvel at your creativity.

Perfect prep

• Sand surfaces lightly to create a 'key' for the paint to adhere to. If the surface already has paint on it, ensure there are no flaky bits after sanding.
• Clean thoroughly with sugar soap and water and leave to dry.
• Prime, ensuring that you use an appropriate primer for the material you are painting (for example, melamine will require a multi-surface primer rather than a wood primer). If you're painting a surface that has been painted before, use an undercoat instead.
• Paint the furniture with an appropriate paint. Eggshell offers a fashionable low sheen yet hardwearing finish, while gloss provides a tougher, shinier result. For a flat matt, vintage-style finish, try chalk paint, which won't require any surface prep but must be sealed with a wax coat.

Tip

Wrap paintbrushes in cling film while you wait for coats to dry, and choose water-based rather than oil-based paint, for easier cleaning.

1

As a renter, how can I make my home feel like my own?

In brief: Opt for a 'love the one you're with' approach, using creative workarounds and disguises to get things as close to your tastes as financially and logistically possible

When you're in a temporary home – whether it's not your own at all, or you feel it's a stopgap to something bigger and better – there are understandably limitations to how much you want (and are allowed) to do to modify the space. This is particularly true if you are on a short-term tenancy. A key rule to remember is to pick your battles: realistically, you won't be installing bi-fold doors or remodelling the entire bathroom, so focus your efforts where you can achieve the best results on a reasonable budget.

If your rental is unfurnished, invest in good, neutral basics that should see you through future homes, such as a bed and a sofa, then jazz things up with a cool collection of cushions or a quirky coffee table. If you have to work around your landlord's furniture, all is not lost. Disguise is your best friend if you don't like what you see, so pile on the throws and tablecloths (which can hide a multitude of sins – not just tables), or even experiment with temporary surface coverings, such as sticky-backed plastic.

Adding colour to walls is one of the most transformative things you can do for minimal outlay, but if you're not able to paint, think outside the box by 'decorating' with colourful strips of removable washi tape or vinyl wall stickers (plenty of designs and patterns are available, or make your own with cut-out vinyl shapes). Art is another crucial element in making a house feel like a home. If you stick to lightweight, frameless prints, you might get away with 'hanging' them from bulldog clips or vintage trouser hangers attached to the wall with sticky tack. Framed art is still an option, even if you're not allowed to make holes in your walls, if you use removable Velcro or sticky picture-hanging strips to fix it up. Wall-mounted shelving will probably fall into the same must-not-make-holes category, but stacking crates will give you the flexibility to add or subtract what you need to suit your space and storage requirements. Finally, never underestimate the power of good accessories. Just as a piece of statement jewellery can transform an otherwise plain outfit, so a strategically placed decorative object can help to pull together a bland or less-than-lovely room.

If surface space is limited, you could ask your landlord whether you can fit a row of picture ledges in key places, which can be left in situ when you move on. These will allow you to be flexible with your displays throughout your tenancy, while minimizing wall damage, and can usually be sourced cheaply.

My pet's paraphernalia is so ugly!

In brief: Work with your pet's natural desire for a cosy nook and tuck things away tidily

Nothing makes a house a home quite like sharing it with a four-legged furry companion, but their bits and bobs can swiftly take over – and they aren't always pretty. Splashing out on designer pet beds is one approach, but with a bit of savvy styling, some clever shopping and even a bit of DIY you can come up with something to do the job at a fraction of the cost.

It's important for pets to feel that they have a 'safe space' to act as a cosy retreat. Dog or cat crates work well, and, luckily for the sake of aesthetics, they are most effective when tucked away in a corner and dressed with blankets to increase the denlike feel. Place a pretty throw over the top or craft a fitted cover from some favourite fabric. You could even treat the crate as a piece of furniture, tucking it under a shelf, side table or baby-changing trolley, with the bonus that there will be space above to store your pet's food and toys. A similar approach can be used to house cat litter trays, providing felines with a little privacy to do their business while keeping their 'offerings' out of sight.

As with children, it's advisable not to give pets access to all their toys all the time, so keep most tucked away but close at hand in a stylish blanket basket or storage chest. In the kitchen, decant food and treats into airtight storage jars, vintage biscuit tins or old tea caddies to keep them accessible without compromising on appearance; just ensure that all family members know where they are. Setting up a pet feeding station can also help to minimize the likelihood of half-eaten bowls of kibble being kicked across the kitchen floor. You could convert the base of a kitchen island to hold food and water bowls securely, or cut holes into a low, free-standing bench, crate or shelf. Finally, get organized by fixing up a dedicated pet hook for collars, leads and other walkwear items to prevent the spread of detritus and get you out of the door efficiently.

Above left: An otherwise redundant kitchen cupboard could easily be converted into a doggy hidey-hole (and allows your pup to remain tucked out of the way yet still on hand to help 'tidy up' any dropped food remnants). Just remove the door and kit it out with a comfy bed.

Above right: Certain furniture (like side tables, coffee tables or armchairs) by its nature tends to incorporate 'dead' space in the lower half, which can offer a canny spot to situate a bijou pet house. If DIY isn't your thing, shop around for a chic dog bed or cat pod to perfectly fit underneath your item.

Below: The silhouette of a traditional doghouse has a certain charm, and constructing something simple in the same shape could make for a chic and cosy indoor pet bedroom, particularly if it uses on-trend woods such as ply. If you work out your dimensions, you could get a local DIY store to cut the pieces you need to size, before screwing it together yourself.

What can I do to avoid faddy decor?

In brief: Start with the basics and work your way up, using trends as an accent rather than the main event

Fashion and interiors have always gone more or less hand in hand, although the former understandably moves more quickly. While many of us want our interiors to look current, we can't be expected to re-tile our bathrooms every six months to match the latest tones. The key to creating a timeless home with integrity, yet which still feels relevant, is to sniff out what's a flash-in-the-pan trend and what might be a slower lifestyle shift, and work accordingly, while leaving as much future-proofing wiggle room as possible.

Start with the bare bones, since they're key to creating a neutral canvas. If you keep flooring relatively classic, for example, you will reap the benefits in the long term (herringbone wooden floors, encaustic patterned tiles and natural sisal carpeting are all beautiful and stylish, yet timeless). If you're keen on a bold, brash floor pattern, do it with rugs instead. Kitchen and bathroom trends tend to evolve rather than emerge, and period styles and a more natural, mismatched feel have lately been replacing high-gloss, fully fitted units. One could arguably call this a trend, too, but it's an approach that feels more forgiving, and is easily adaptable once the fashion moves on.

Vintage also comes in waves. Antique 'brown' furniture has fallen out of favour in recent years (although it can work wonderfully if given a simple paint job), while the shabby-chic trend reached saturation point several years ago and is now looking increasingly dated. Mid-Century design, on the other hand, seems to have persisted quietly throughout, and its elegant, timeless shapes still appear as contemporary as they did in the 1950s. Counting on its continuing longevity seems a relatively safe bet, and investing in a classic Ercol bench or G Plan dining set and mixing it with trend-led cushions or crockery will strike just the right tone. Colour trends come and go, of course, so it's wise to allow your property itself to influence your choices. Muted tones with a grey pigment provide easy-to-live-with sophistication that will complement a period space, while a modern home can better tolerate cleaner, more saturated colours. Pick the base colour carefully, then add bolder accents throughout or in rooms that you can redecorate easily.

This dining area offers a masterclass in timeless style with a bit of a bite: Victorian details such as a ceiling rose and cornicing mingle effortlessly with contemporary drop pendants and a Mid-Century dining table set, while a raised kitchen island all but makes the kitchen beyond invisible. Textural elements like the simple rag-style rug help to soften all the hard materials.

Tip

Still struggling to tell what's a passing trend? Take a look at Pinterest and Instagram: if they have become awash with pineapple motifs and unicorn heads, say, avoid using those for anything other than fun accents.

Help! We've a baby on the way ... and we live in a one-bedroom flat

In brief: Create a 'baby station' as a one-stop shop for all your changing needs, hide toys in grown-up storage, and worry about the rest once they're a bit bigger

Kids undoubtedly require a lot of kit, but, at least initially, they don't take up much room themselves. So don't panic! The early days will be a sleep-starved blur of little more than eating, napping and, um, the other, so making the essentials streamlined and accessible will help to smooth things over. You'll need a cot, of course, although you don't even need that at the very beginning if you plan on using a co-sleeper at first. Moses baskets are another option for those early weeks, but do bear in mind that they won't be any use after a few months, so if storage is limited, a flat-pack crib might be a more practical option.

It makes sense to keep all changing items (and ideally clothing, too) in one place, but there's no reason it has to be in your bedroom. Dedicating a sturdy piece of furniture, such as a chest of drawers or a sideboard, keeps all the basics confined to one area. When baby is tiny, you can even use the top to change them on, with a cot-top baby changer (never leave them unattended while using it, of course), otherwise it can house their mat ready for moving to a bed or the floor when required. Decanting everyday essentials such as nappies, muslin cloths and cotton-wool balls looks prettier and makes them more accessible: use clear containers (avoid glass in case of knocks) or chic storage baskets to tie in with the rest of your interiors scheme. Wall-mounted shelving or even hanging baskets will help to keep surfaces clear.

Rather than a nursing chair, which can be cumbersome, a retro-style rocker for feeding offers comfort for you and baby, as well as blending seamlessly into a living space. Ensure that it's equipped with cushions and throws, plus a small side table for cups of tea and baby bottles. Speaking of throws, invest in several cheap ones to chuck over that deeply impractical velvet sofa or your best bedlinen at a moment's notice. Design-wise, don't feel pressurized to kit everywhere out in garish, themed kiddie prints. For babies under three months old, monochrome schemes with contrasting patterns are the most appealing, and they're far more aesthetically pleasing to adults than pirate or princess motifs.

See also page 128: Is it possible to create a tasteful children's room?

A baby station like this is fairly imperative in a small flat, but it could also be a useful downstairs addition to a larger home, alongside a separate set of changing equipment upstairs.

How can I customize my chain-store kitchen cabinets?

In brief: Cover up what you don't like, add individual or luxury elements to break things up, and think of cupboard handles as jewellery

If you're not in a position to change your kitchen, or are after a quick fix to tide you over before refitting the space completely, you can drastically change its appearance without expending much time or money. Painting the cabinets is a good first step, and can give dated wooden doors a contemporary look, as well as providing an opportunity to introduce colour. Most standard kitchen units are constructed from engineered wood particleboard with a melamine veneer, leading many people to believe that they can't be painted, but with the right primer and paint even high-gloss doors can be transformed (see page 46 for how to paint melamine surfaces, among others).

If you're feeling adventurous, consider cladding your cupboard doors. This is most easily done if they don't have mouldings. Visit your local builders' merchant and get thin wooden boards cut to the same size as your existing doors, then fix them in place with wood glue. Get experimental and try using pegboard, oriented strand board (OSB) or plywood for a contemporary look, finishing with a clear waterproof varnish for practicality. If that's scared you off completely though, get in touch with a company that specializes in replacement cupboard doors, and simply change old for new while retaining the original cupboard carcasses.

Another antidote to the chain-store blah is to add something bespoke. This needn't mean splashing the cash on custom carpentry, since personalization can come in many forms. You could remove the doors from the wall cupboards altogether to create open shelving, adding decorative wallpaper to the backs of the cupboards for a splash of pattern. Or mix things up with shelving made from reclaimed wood to contrast with your contemporary cabinets. An unexpected element, such as a vintage ladder used to suspend plants or pots and pans, can be enough to distract from basic cabinetry and create an individual look. Finally, don't overlook the importance of great door handles, which really can elevate a scheme.

See also page 30: Am I stuck with my existing wall tiles?

This delicate mint-green tone offers an unexpected pop of colour in an otherwise neutral kitchen. Simple holes can be an elegant and affordable alternative to drawer handles, and they are easily made using a spade bit attached to a drill. Here, the extractor fan has been boxed in, but you can also use heat-resistant appliance paint on an exposed cooker hood to help it blend in with the rest of the kitchen.

Do I really need to make a moodboard?

In brief: It can help – but think of it more as a useful collection of references than as a polished presentation

There seems to be a trend of late for almost 'competitive' moodboarding, the goal of which is a beautiful moodboard in itself, rather than a tool to help you achieve your desired result. This can make the whole idea seem superfluous and daunting – and a little over the top if you're just trying to redecorate your downstairs loo. Even so, the moodboard remains a useful way of helping you hone your ideas and avoid making costly design mistakes. In our digital age, touching tangible samples and physically seeing paint colours and finishes together in the flesh can be very helpful.

If you're not sure where to start, try making a 'vision' board. This is useful for getting to know your tastes and ideas before you become bogged down in the nitty-gritty of matching carpets with curtains. It should help you to pinpoint the overall effect you want to create, rather than the specific look. There are no real rules: pick up a pile of magazines, postcards or old photos and pull out images that you're drawn to, or that make you happy. These could be a pattern formed by shadows or an abstract artwork, even physical pieces such as an old bit of driftwood or some amazing packaging, rather than anything related specifically to interiors. Find something you can fix everything to, for easy reference – a large sheet of card will do, or a cork board. If you've got an empty piece of wall in a spare room, you could even tack everything to that, and place physical objects on a shelf or surface in front of it.

This can be a rather less overwhelming starting point from which to hone your ideas into a room-specific moodboard, with the overall 'vision board' serving as a multi-room tool. Start by pulling out key elements that you'd like to feature in your scheme, then think about how they could translate to your specific room; a predilection for seascapes, for example, could translate into a cool, natural space with rustic painted furniture and dip-dyed curtains. Gradually move towards looking at real samples of important elements such as tiles or paint, and you should be well on your way to a successful and coherent scheme.

See also page 6: I just got the keys – now what?

If you're creating your moodboard directly onto a wall – or aren't quite ready to commit to the permanence of glue on a board – a low-tack tape such as washi or some masking tape can be the perfect tool for the job. Keep things quite tightly packed, so you have space to expand outwards as you find further inspiration.

INTERIOR DESIGN RULES: Which to follow and which to break

They say rules were made to be broken, but in order to do that, you must know them in the first place. Here are five common interior design truisms, and how to interpret them to make them work for you.

1. They say: Follow the 60/30/10 rule when choosing colours. Sixty per cent of the room should contain the dominant colour and thirty per cent the secondary colour, leaving ten per cent for accent pieces. **We say**: Loosely following this makes sense – since going all-out colour crazy can result in a frenetic, disjointed feel, especially if you're not sure what you're doing – but don't let it bog you down. Sometimes the most successful schemes are those that incorporate 'a little bit of wrong', which actually gives depth and soul to a space.

2. They say: Use symmetry to create a balanced space. **We say**: It's true that our brains are programmed to find symmetry pleasing, even therapeutic. But too much of it in a small space can feel bland and dull, and possibly even overwhelming. Try using a symmetrical approach with key elements or focal points - a circular table directly in the centre of a square room, for example – but break it up with an off-centre sideboard or ornaments arranged together in odd numbers.

3. They say: Decorate with natural colours. **We say**: Mother Nature is not to be trifled with, and she certainly knows what she's doing, though 'natural' certainly needn't mean neutral. Look at the way she balances hues and proportions (in fact, we think she might be following the 60/30/10 rule), whether it's in the sombre, muted tones of a stormy sky or the vibrant, unexpected contrasts of a bird of paradise.

4. They say: Choose furniture and flooring that are proportionate to the size of the room. **We say**: Common wisdom might dictate that the smaller the room, the more diminutive the objects you should put in it, but in fact this can create a cluttered, broken look. Think less, but bigger: go bold and choose a show-stopping L-shaped sofa over a two-seater and armchairs to act as a bold and inviting focal point, for example. The same rule can be applied to flooring, using large-format tiles or wide planks.

5. They say: Stick to white or light tones in a small space. **We say**: While white seems an obvious choice - it reflects light and brightens dark corners - there's also a danger that it will feel bland, and if there's not enough to attract the eye the space will ultimately still look small (albeit pale). A vibrant hue might not be to everyone's taste, but it can give a luxurious jewellery-box vibe, while dark tones add atmosphere and mood as well as highlighting interesting architectural details, creating an inviting sanctuary.

1

How can I give my tired old sofa a new lease of life?

In brief: Fix any faults, then dress it up to the nines

There's something about a sad, saggy sofa that brings down the entire look of a room. If a new model isn't on the cards though, there is still plenty you can do on a limited budget to spruce up your downcast seating.

First, obliterate that sag. Most sofas and armchairs have seat pads (and some have back pads) that you can unzip. If the pads really are on their last legs, you may need to replace the foam completely, but for most sofas, some sneaky top-up padding will do. Adding pieces of foam from a mattress topper or similar to the top and bottom of your existing pad can make a big difference (trace around the cushion pad to make a template), or simply use upholstery wadding to pack out the sagging areas around the cushion pad while it's inside its cover. The same can be done with shabby scatter cushions.

Of equal importance is the upholstery. Making professionally fitted covers is a skilled job, but if your sofa has fabric covers – and if you can use a sewing machine – it's possible to tackle it yourself. By removing the old covers and using them as a template, you can make your own in their exact size and shape, then use a staple gun to secure the new upholstery underneath the bottom of the sofa. There are non-sewing options, too: depending on the shape of your sofa, you may be able to fashion some fabric to fit its frame simply with strategic folding and a staple gun. Otherwise, tucking a throw neatly into the frame of the sofa will offer instant improvement; place the seat pads on top of the throw to stop it from falling down. If your sofa covers are machine-washable, a machine dye could give them a dramatic new look for relatively little money and effort. This does depend on the type, weight and original colour of the fabric, however, so be guided by the dye manufacturer's instructions.

Now that the sofa itself is looking a little brighter, it's time for some layering, for the final flourish: cushions and throws add texture and interest, and a blanket draped delicately over a cat-scratched or grubby arm will hide a multitude of sins. Choose an uneven number of cushions in various sizes for a considered yet casual look.

Above: Layering fabric over the sofa and down to the floor creates a valance effect that can be helpful to hide ugly sofa legs or to use the space underneath for storage. The cushions are in a mix of styles and colours, but the harmonious palette of greens and blues ensures they don't look messy. Pops of red are used as an accent.

Below left: Natural fabrics such as linen, denim and wool can be hardwearing yet beautiful for covering sofas and chairs, especially when used in a setting with other natural elements such as oak beams or floorboards.

Below right: Unexpected fabrics can create an interesting finish for soft furnishings. Here, antique lace layered over a neutral sofa gives a vintage touch and suits the ethereal whiteness of the room.

Tip

Did you know that you can paint your fabric sofa? Mix chalk paint and water in equal parts and apply to the fabric with a brush, using a spray bottle of water as you go to keep the fabric wet. Use a circular motion to work the paint in thoroughly, and fine-grade sandpaper to rough up the surface gently after each coat (two to four coats should be enough). Finish by working clear wax into the fabric with a rag or brush. This technique works best on fabrics with minimal pattern or texture. It might initially feel a little rough but should soften with use (a patch test first would be advisable).

I'm a collector - how can I best display my prized possessions?

In brief: As the young folk say: go hard, or go home

Collections often come about organically. You find yourself drawn to a particular type of object and accrue a few, then friends and family start giving them to you, and before you know it it's a 'thing'. If you're not careful, it could tip from 'collection' into 'hoarding' and even make you fall out of love with it in the first place. Whatever you collect, embrace it wholeheartedly (while being mindful of the hoarder aspect) and celebrate it as worthy of adoration, even if it happens to be 1950s milk cartons rather than rare Fabergé eggs.

The type of object will, of course, play an important part in how you display it, but as a general rule grouped collections pack the strongest punch visually and are more effective than if you disperse pieces here and there. Think of these trinkets and treasures as a three-dimensional story rather than simply decor, and your job is to help them to shine. Artwork or framed objects are fairly straightforward to deal with, since they will by their nature hang on the wall. Play around with the arrangement on the floor before you fix anything up, and keep in mind that you may need to leave space to accommodate more examples. Keeping some element of cohesion - all black frames or uniformity of spacing, perhaps - will strengthen the curated vibe.

Physical objects must be curated a little more thoughtfully. Tiny pieces might sit together sweetly on a spice rack or picture ledge (you could even play with positioning, so that they look as though they're interacting with one another), while a collection of crystals could be arranged in ways that are appropriate to the qualities of the particular stones, as well as in an aesthetically pleasing way, such as inside terrariums. Collections don't have to be limited to a particular type of object, of course; they could be anything that you notice has a clear common thread, such as a rusty industrial patina or a single colour tone. Whatever your collection, if you stick to these rules you should successfully avoid the nutty professor effect.

See also page 132: I'm a terrible hoarder - how can I clear the clutter?

Above left: A collection of coloured glassware can look particularly striking when placed in front of a window or other light source, allowing the light to shine through and create interesting shadows and twinkles within the room.

Above right: Going graphic can instantly give a modern feel to a collection, even one wholly consisting of vintage or antique pieces. By using a perfectly level hanging line and arranging by size, this humble collection of scissors forms a beguiling display.

Below: Old printer's trays can offer great display space for tiny trinkets when wall mounted or leaned upright on a surface. Keep an eye out for them at car boot sales, vintage stores and online auction sites.

My kitchen is my living space

In brief: Arrange furniture to define different functions within the space, and/or disguise your kitchen a little

Many new apartments or converted flats feature an 'open-plan' kitchen and living area, but reading between the lines of the estate agent's spiel, this often means a kitchen with a sofa tucked into a corner, or a living room with a couple of kitchen cupboards and a sink along the back wall. There are two ways to deal with this dilemma, and the one you choose will depend on how much space you have to play with: zone things out to create separate areas, or treat the decor as one overall room, sticking to a cohesive scheme throughout. The former can be wise if you have some space, while the latter is advisable for a genuinely tiny area.

Luckily, the larger furniture that you're likely to have in this room anyway – such as a sofa or dining table – works really well to create natural barriers between different areas and functions. If you can, use a dining table (or raised bench acting as a kitchen island or breakfast bar) to bridge the gap between cooking and leisure, and ideally place your main sofa or seating away from the kitchen, so that you're not staring directly at your dirty dishes when you're trying to unwind of an evening. Play up this zoning by giving each area its own identity – a grounding rug and strong artwork in the living section, or a dining table made from a contrasting material to the kitchen worktops, for example.

Blending your kitchen in can also help, whatever the size of the room. Consider a semi-fitted kitchen, comprising free-standing or mismatched furniture alongside built-in cupboards, for a more homely feel, or fit shelving rather than wall units, and style them with the odd decorative item as well as crockery and foodstuffs. A pantry or fold-back cabinet doors can hide all kinds of things, including less-than-lovely items such as the microwave. In particularly small spaces, sticking to a limited palette of colours and materials is easier on the eye and will help things flow. For example, if you're using pale wood for the kitchen cabinetry, carry it through into your coffee table and other smaller pieces. Ensuring that there is some sort of design correlation among all the elements will create a cohesive rather than disjointed effect.

See also page 20: Should I go open-plan?

Above: Within this predominantly white space, a striking shade of aqua has been cleverly incorporated into the bones of the room itself, from the stair risers to light fixtures, as well as in accent pieces, encouraging the eye to travel around the overall area.

Below: Despite the sofa's close proximity to the kitchen area, it faces away from both the kitchen and dining spaces, providing an element of separation. The back of the sofa also creates a corridor feel within the kitchen, which helps to visually separate the spaces further.

Tip

If you're in a studio flat, try to situate your sleeping area as far from the kitchen as possible, and mark it out as a separate area using a curtain or wide set of shelves. The novelty of making tea and toast directly from your bed will wear off quickly.

Our household is busy (read: messy) – I need it to be chaos-proof!

In brief: Choose hardwearing and wipe-clean options for everything from floor coverings to furniture, and set up some organizational systems to help keep things under control

Our homes have to stand up to a lot: muddy dogs, wayward toddlers with a propensity to chuck spaghetti at the walls, and a myriad other daily assaults. Choosing clever decorative finishes is one way to minimize damage. Hardwearing flooring is crucial, so stick to solid wood, laminate or tiles for easy mopping. You could even use an alternative such as rubber, which comes in a plethora of colours and is extremely durable, or, for a touch of industrial chic, finish an existing concrete sub-floor with stain or sealant and leave uncovered. For walls and woodwork, silk or satin paint is more hardwearing than matt, or make life even easier for yourself by choosing paint with a wipe-clean finish or decorating with water-resistant vinyl wallpaper.

As the saying goes, a place for everything and everything in its place. Putting baskets, trays and bowls for 'things to go elsewhere' in key areas (notably the top and bottom of staircases and in family rooms) can help you to achieve that goal, as a stopgap before things actually get put in their place. Storage is crucial in entrance spaces, to stop chaos from spreading. Ensure that each family member has their own hook and a place to store their shoes, and be ruthless about putting out-of-season stuff away.

Pull together a core cleaning kit, separate from your general cleaning supplies, and make sure it's easily accessible and can be grabbed at a moment's notice (a cordless vacuum and spray mop can be particularly useful, and having a good multi-purpose spray and selection of cleaning cloths and sponges to hand is invaluable in an emergency). For 'brain cleansing', make sure there's an area for mental clutter, for use by the whole family, with space for a shopping list and calendar and somewhere to pin invitations, thoughts and notes. A cork board is a good bet, and if you have space you could take it a step further and cover a whole alcove in cork tiles, or coat a wall (or door) in magnetic chalkboard paint. Alternatively, a run of pretty clipboards, with one assigned to each family member, can offer useful space for holding notes and papers.

In high-traffic areas such as a hallway, painting the wall below the dado rail in a dark tone, or covering it in a textured wallpaper, will make scuffs less noticeable than a pristine pale surface. If you don't have a dado, simply paint to a neat line instead.

How do I tackle my north-facing room?*

In brief: Work with its inherent gloom, transforming it into a cosy cave

North-facing rooms are notoriously unpopular with designers. Unlike their easy-going south-facing counterparts, which smugly handle just about any colour scheme you throw at them, north-facing spaces have their own list of special requirements. These rooms receive cool and unforgiving light, and if colour and design schemes aren't modified accordingly the result can be an equally cool and unforgiving space. Choosing a white or pale tint might seem sensible, but in reality the lack of sharp shadows can make it feel rather dead. Conversely, a deeper or darker hue can create a surprisingly comforting and cocooning space, where the fact that less light is being bounced around works in its favour to blur the edges of the room.

Rather than try to fight what nature has thrown at you, pick up the ball and run with it. Depending on which room it is, pile textured throws and knitted cushions on your sofa, bring in sumptuous fabrics such as velvet for window treatments or use a linen tablecloth for a dining area. Whether for walls or furnishings, choose colours with a warm yellow base to fight off the chill. Be clever with where you place the colour, too: in a long, thin room, a dark tone on the opposing long walls can help to emphasize the length, drawing the eye along, and sticking to lighter colours and materials around a window can trick the eye into reading the surrounding area as a source of light, along with the window itself.

Don't forget to use tester pots before committing to any paint colour. The light coming into the room will alter the way the colour appears at different times of day, and that will in turn have an impact on your furnishings (for example, a neutral with green undertones may turn out cooler than you imagined, and if your furniture is in a warm hue, the result will be less than harmonious). Consider the effect artificial light has on the space, since you will spend a chunk of your time there outside daylight hours.

* Or south-facing room in the southern hemisphere.

This dark space really goes for it with both dark walls and furniture, yet the warmth in these tones brings a real richness. By balancing things out with a light rug and white accents throughout the space, the overall look is powerful, but not overwhelming.

Tip

Fancy doing something sneaky? Try painting the hallway or landing directly outside the room in a much darker tone, to trick the eye into thinking the space is lighter than it is as you enter.

I've got no built-in storage (and can't add any)

In brief: Optimize the free-standing storage you have, and try a few clever hacks to make the most of difficult corners

Getting your hands on a property that is already equipped with brilliant built-in storage can be akin to finding the Holy Grail, particularly if you're not in a position to install anything permanent yourself. While free-standing pieces are undoubtedly useful and do sometimes offer the best option, there's no denying that a house without a scrap of cupboard space – particularly if it has awkward nooks and crannies – can be frustrating and impractical.

It's wise to make the most of what you've got. Adding storage baskets or characterful vintage suitcases to the tops of free-standing furniture (or sliding them underneath) makes maximum use of dead space within the same footprint. Put the storage you do have to best use, either by adding smaller storage baskets inside or installing more (or fewer) shelves, depending on what you want to store. Repurposing pieces can work well; a large old wardrobe could be placed in a dining room, for example, and fitted with shelving to store extra crockery and baking equipment, and will probably cost a lot less than a purpose-built cabinet of the same size.

If you're buying new pieces, aim for ones that have a dual use. A long storage bench makes a great banquette in a dining area, rather than ordinary chairs, and an old trunk in place of a coffee table can store all manner of family detritus. How about a row of slim vintage school lockers in the hallway? Think creatively: a stack of old trunks will add a talking point as well as valuable storage space in an awkward corner, and if you use luggage labels to list what each one holds, and place occasional items in the lower trunks, it is eminently practical. Think small, too, with clever little household hacks: a magnetic strip stuck to a bathroom wall can be an ingenious place to store hair grips, nail clippers and tweezers in one spot while taking up hardly any space, or slide a slim trolley into an end-of-unit gap in your kitchen to house cleaning products.

See also page 8: Should I go for built-in or free-standing furniture?

The humble apple crate can be put to myriad uses: designed to be strong and sturdy, they make great shelf and storage space and can usually be sourced relatively inexpensively at reclamation yards or vintage stores. By cleverly arranging them inside an understairs alcove here, both the crates themselves and the negative spaces provided in between them offer an eminently workable storage solution in an otherwise awkward area.

STYLISH STORAGE: Ways to add chic stowaway spots

Outside-the-box thinking can be useful when it comes to storage (even if it yields some box-based solutions). Here are five creative ideas for housing and displaying pretty and practical bits and bobs.

1. Converted crate

Old fruit crates or their shallow sisters, drinks crates, have durability in their DNA. Whether free-standing or wall-mounted, solo or in a row, they add strength and character to any space. Some come with their original dividers, which, when the crate is stood on its side, offer practical shelving for smaller items, but it's possible to add some if yours doesn't. Take suitably sized timber battens, saw them to size and attach them to the inside of your crate, fixing them with screws from the outside or mini brackets from within.

2. Drinks cabinet as shelving unit

Once de rigueur in any home, the intrinsically glamorous cocktail cabinet is no longer such a household essential (although that other retro favourite, the bar cart, has steadily been gaining momentum of late). These beautiful cabinets can easily be put to good alternative use, however, to house a myriad pieces worthy of display. A collection of some sort is an obvious example, but for something a little more unexpected, use a drinks cabinet to house shoes, turning your favourite heels into design statements while keeping them accessible.

3. Vintage suitcases

Let's face it, as lovely as they look, we're not keen to go back to lugging these vintage beauties through the departure lounge when we've got fancy quadruple-wheeled versions in the loft. But old cases are undeniably sturdy and full of character, not to mention easy to find (often for a steal) at second-hand shops. Stack some in a corner to house spare towels, bedlinen, out-of-season clothing and anything else you can think of.

4. Vintage ladder as occasional storage

Old wooden ladders are usually full of charm and can make a versatile, unexpectedly useful addition to the home. Use one as a makeshift bookcase when you need a little extra storage, and if it's still sound and you have limited space to keep a functional ladder elsewhere, you can simply empty it next time you need to change a lightbulb.

5. Spice racks

Spice racks offer small, inexpensive, slim shelving that can be invaluable for housing small decorative objects. Place one in the bathroom for storing a collection of colour-blocked nail varnishes; put one in a child's room for their favourite collectible action figurines; or use one to show off your favourite book covers or even in place of a picture ledge, for an informal approach to displaying artwork.

1

I love the industrial warehouse style ... but I live in a suburban semi

In brief: See what you can unearth beneath the surface, or cheat your way to the look with clever fakery

Not since *Flashdance* has industrial been so chic, and developers of old industrial conversions are falling over themselves to preserve original details and boost the desirability of their properties. It's easy to achieve that industrial style without it looking like a themed set, if you keep a little integrity. Columns, beams, concrete and bare brickwork typify the style, and they can be found and revealed in a variety of homes, even if they are hidden under neat plasterboard and carpeting. The restrained colour palette found in many warehouse homes – black, white and grey, warmed up with rustic wood – can be surprisingly cosy and easy to live with in smaller spaces.

Consider stripping back elements of your space to allow its inner workings to become part of the decor. An old wall with its original bricks, naturally patinated plaster or even fragments of old wallpaper can be a striking feature, especially if you contrast it with crisp paintwork elsewhere. Leaving copper pipes on show can offer a nod to industrial spaces, as can leaving structural support beams such as RSJs uncovered. Original floorboards work perfectly, too; if your home doesn't have any, seek out a solid wood or laminate with a rough-sawn finish. You can even cheat your way to the look by gently ageing new boards, a process that is somewhat trial and error but can be very effective: stain or paint the boards in various tones and sand them back in places until you're happy with the result.

If there really is nothing exciting lurking in your space, fear not and fake it. Brick slips create a realistic stripped-brick effect, and you can give them an aged, distressed look by sponging on a watered-down whitewash unevenly. Products such as Microscreed (for the effect of polished concrete) and Tadelakt (a plaster finish) create a durable finish that can work particularly well in wet areas such as kitchens and bathrooms. Or have fun with a *trompe-l'œil* wallpaper that mimics raw concrete or rustic tin tiles, for a tongue-in-cheek hint of industry in a modern space. Reclaimed materials can help you to get the look; think old scaffolding boards transformed into shelving or original factory pendant lighting in a contemporary new-build.

Above: This converted ground-floor flat mixes many typical industrial elements with aplomb, resulting in an aesthetic akin to a cosy yet cool gastropub. Exposed pipework and industrial materials are warmed by the liberal use of salvaged warm woods and a characterful old Chesterfield.

Below left: Galvanized steel pipes and pipe fittings are used to create this immensely practical and hardwearing shelving. If creating this look is beyond your skills remit, a local builder might be able to install something similar.

Below right: Leaving a single wall unfinished gives a unique and characterful quality to a space. To ward off dust, brush on a terracotta sealant after cleaning the wall thoroughly.

How do I bring light into my windowless bathroom?

In brief: Get clever with artificial lighting and use walls, fixtures and fittings to bounce the light you *do* have into all the right places

Rooms with no windows can feel claustrophobic if they are not cleverly decorated, but a lack of windows isn't a barrier to a successful bathroom scheme; you just have to be careful. The principal aim is to distract the eye from the fact that there is no natural light, so that it's not even noticeable until it dawns almost as an afterthought.

Artificial lighting is crucial, of course. Recessed ceiling lights provide practical all-round illumination without feeling as stark as a single, central source, and supplementary lighting around the sink (even integrated into a mirrored cabinet, for a soft ambience) can provide a shadow-free glow to aid shaving or applying make-up. You might be able to sneak additional lighting into other clever spots, such as incorporating SELV (safety extra-low voltage) LED lighting strips low down (in the base of a bath or vanity unit, say) to give a gentle wash of light over the floor.

Warm white bulbs or LEDs are more accommodating than cool-hued ones, and allow you to be bold with wall colours, whether through paint, tiles or even wallpaper. Satin paint, glossy tiles or wallpaper with a natural sheen help to bounce what light there is around the space. Use them to add focal points: mixing differently coloured mosaic tiles in random configurations throughout the space, say, or painting flashes of vibrant colour in specific spots or using a heavily patterned wallpaper to draw the eye to a particular area. Frameless or even mirrored-glass shower doors or screens will also allow the eye to move freely around the space.

Large mirrors or even artwork can also help to distract, especially in a space where one might expect a window to be. While a decent mirror above the sink is essential, an additional arrangement of smaller, mismatched vintage ones elsewhere can confuse the eye as to where the room actually ends. A bold framed print will give the punch of character that such a space needs (just avoid placing it where it might get wet, and ensure that it's in a decent frame and behind glass). Of course, if the lack of light really bothers you, you could always look into installing a sun pipe or skylight, should the architecture allow.

See also page 124: My lighting feels stark – how can I soften it?

Above left: A large sheet of mirror glass fitted directly to the wall can be a canny space-bending trick, especially if it wraps across the whole wall. If this isn't an option, seek out a large, fuss-free bevelled mirror to fit the space instead.

Above right: Painting walls with the darkest of hues can actually cause them to recess visually, and paired with glossy white tiles and sanitaryware it gives an uplifting feel. Sticking to monochrome looks simple yet striking; alternatively use the dark background as a foil for bright pops of colour.

Below: The liberal use of mirrors and shiny surfaces helps bounce the light around this space (and the available light itself is also plentiful, thanks to clever strip lighting alongside a central ceiling light). The bold artwork naturally draws the eye, as a window would.

Tip

Certain requirements have to be met for lighting installed around baths or showers and other water sources. In the UK, for example, bathroom lighting is IP (ingress protection) rated, a numbering system that determines the protection offered against immersion in water. Find details, or equivalent information for other countries, online.

My space is too big!

In brief: All right, there's no need to brag …
meet your new best friend, zoning

While it might elicit little sympathy from those with a shoebox of a home, an excessively large living space does come with its own set of problems. Think of your design 'job' as creating smaller pockets within the main space, whether visually or literally. The former approach is where zoning comes in; this involves grouping furniture according to function (for instance, an oversized sofa and armchairs centred on a rug to form a cosy sitting area). Placing key furniture with its backs to other parts of the room can help increase a feeling of intimacy by reducing how much of the space you can see. Even large potted plants can help to separate things visually; choose tall varieties, such as the fiddle-leaf fig tree, for maximum impact. Whatever you do, don't line everything up against the walls – it'll feel sterile.

If you choose the literal approach, use large free-standing pieces of furniture (sets of open shelves and long console tables are useful because they still allow light through), or even sliding doors, paper screens or curtains fixed to a ceiling-mounted track, to demarcate the various areas. There's no reason you can't place a tall cupboard or wardrobe so that its back faces into a room, almost acting like a partition wall; if the back isn't pretty, paint it or cover it with wallpaper, or even hang pictures on it. As a rule of thumb, stick to using fewer but larger – even oversized – pieces of furniture, and maintain a consistent sense of scale. Try not to over-fill the space: a couple of huge L-shaped sofas with a statement armchair will look more cohesive than a collection of smaller seats (and the 'L' could also act as a room divider of sorts, doing two jobs in one).

Flooring can also define and demarcate a space, so play with boundaries to create different areas visually. This needn't involve hard lines; you could use, say, hexagonal floor tiles in one area and stagger their segue into a different type of flooring, for an interesting blend, or stick to the same tiles throughout but alter the colours throughout the room. You can get the same effect on the walls by using punches of bold colour in different parts of the space, to act as visual punctuation in the various zones.

Above: A large rug, big enough to house a sofa, armchair and coffee table, clearly defines this spot as the living and relaxation space within the open-plan room, whereas a smaller one under the coffee table alone just wouldn't have the same effect.

Below: A room as generous as this can accommodate some bold colour choices, which also act as visual markers to zone the space. In high-ceilinged buildings, this approach can offer an interesting alternative to just using colours on walls to create zones.

How can I ensure that my TV doesn't dominate my space?

In brief: Get creative with how you style it to ensure that it's accessible without being the star of the show

Stylists take pains in upmarket interiors shoots to avoid showing TV sets, yet the fact remains that most of us do have one and it has to go somewhere. The best approach is usually to hide it in plain sight.

Placing a TV set against a dark or even black backdrop is one clever way of making it pretty much invisible when it's switched off, and with black walls moving firmly from 'teen goth bedroom' territory into the 'chic interiors' camp, this could be a canny design move as well. Alternatively, distract the eye by nestling the TV among books and ornaments on top of a unit, or surrounded by artworks if it's wall-mounted. Purpose-built TV cabinets are notoriously ugly and, as TV technology becomes smaller and flatter, not always necessary. If you fancy placing your TV in an alcove, incorporate a built-in shelf for it, allowing it to blend in with other objects housed there. A slim sideboard can work well, especially if it has a few sections of open shelving for cable TV boxes and consoles, and you can drill discreet holes in the back to feed cables through. Think creatively, too: rest a flat screen on an old wooden easel in a corner to add character, or inside a repurposed slim piece of furniture such as a vintage wall-mounted gun cabinet, to tuck it out of sight when it's not in use.

Another consideration is your TV set itself, if you're in the market for a new one. Although they are traditionally all-black, it's possible to find slightly more interesting models. Manufacturers are increasingly teaming up with designers to produce sets that can be showcased like any statement object, with mix-and-match components to allow you to create your own metallic, coloured or wood-framed configurations, or wall-mounted units that turn unobtrusively from a TV into a photographic image or artwork at the touch of a button. Whatever you choose, try to keep cables and other paraphernalia as unobtrusive as possible (nothing kills a look like a sea of tangled electric cords). Hide routers or hubs away in small upturned storage boxes, and fix clips at strategic points to guide cables gently out of sight lines and down to sockets, or hide them in paintable cord covers.

Above: It's an uncommon choice, but a white-framed television was clearly the perfect option for this feminine, all-white space, and sits unobtrusively within its designated spot.

Below left: Although the dimensions of TV sets have changed vastly over the decades, sometimes it's possible to find a charming old TV cabinet that can stylishly house a modern unit, even if it's not a perfect fit. A model with doors, like this one, can instantly transform into a sideboard once shut away.

Below right: Spot the screen? A switched-off TV all but vanishes against an equally dark wall, and clever styling of tabletop accessories and surrounding artwork makes it seem like nothing is missing from the scheme.

My house doesn't feel homely

In brief: Don't forget to include those personal effects that add soul, and don't get caught up in over-styling your space

It's very easy to be impressed by a beautifully executed interiors scheme, with nothing out of place, but it does not necessarily mean that the owner or designer has turned the house into a home. Often the most successful schemes are those with something raw, even 'wrong': a few wonky pictures, a mishmash of tableware, the odd casually clashing ornament. These can be the missing touches in a home that might look perfectly pleasant but not feel homely.

This can be a fine line to tread. You want a curated, coordinated look rather than a jumble of styles and ideas, but do keep that line in mind. Generally, you start to cross it when you begin to prioritize style over function, or – conversely – cover the basics without giving any thought to finishing touches. Take the coffee table: leaving it entirely bare when not in use can look a bit stark, so adding a couple of plants or a stack of your favourite books can help bring things to life, but don't get too obsessed with creating the perfect Instagrammable vignette of over-curated objects; you will inevitably end up kicking over coffee cups that you've put on the floor lest you unbalance your tabletop aesthetic.

Consider all the senses, not just sight, when styling your space. Tactility is crucial, so aim to include a good proportion of warm wood or chunky knitted textiles to add physical warmth. And we all know how enticing the smell of freshly baked bread is in a kitchen, so – while clearly you won't be rustling up loaves constantly – don't overlook the comfort that sweet-smelling candles, incense sticks or flowers can bring.

Adding objects that are connected to you personally can transform the way you feel about your space. Apart from the obvious, such as family photographs, make sure there's a liberal scattering of things you love or that evoke happy memories, regardless (within reason) of whether they 'go' with your interior scheme. That old 1970s ceramic horse figurine that you inherited from Granny, a naff fridge magnet from a holiday resort many moons ago, an artwork featuring a favourite quotation – all these will add more to your home than a perfectly coordinating run of specially chosen ornaments ever could.

With an authentic, rustic feel, the look of this dining space is casual and inviting, yet not the sort of thing one could slavishly recreate with a single trip to a chain store. Rather, the secret of its success is the subtler nuances of gathered and made items mixed with handmade pieces for a look that, while not necessarily expensive, is priceless.

I'm furnishing my room from scratch – how do I work out what to put where?

In brief: Grab some graph paper, think about your core requirements and plot things out before splashing any cash

Most of us have some sort of baggage when we arrive at a new property, but if we're furnishing a room fully for the first time – perhaps as a result of upsizing or building an extension – the prospect of working out what goes where can be intimidating. You will presumably have decided on the function of the space, whether it's one or several, so home in on what the most important (or largest) element will be and work from there. A quick scale sketch can be incredibly useful at this stage; don't worry about creating an architect's blueprint, but simply work something out on a piece of graph paper, incorporating the dimensions of the room as well as those of any proposed furniture.

The flow of space through the room is just as important as whether a piece of furniture physically fits. It is crucial to have enough space to move freely – no one wants to be banging their shins on an inappropriately placed table every time they try to leave the room – so make sure your plans include enough space between furniture.

Seating should be close enough for conversation without feeling nose to nose with your guests, and it should relate to the features of the room, for instance being arranged around a fireplace, overlooking a picture window or – less romantically – pointing at the TV. If there is no natural focal point, create one by installing some statement artwork or setting up a display cabinet. Avoid taking the 'easy' option of placing everything against the walls unless your room really is tiny. Pulling furniture into the centre of a room, or even just angling it outwards, can give a dynamic twist to a space. Placing pieces of furniture so that they face away from one another can feel awkward (unless you're trying to zone an open-plan space). Once you've decided on the main elements, think about accent pieces, and assess what you've got space for: could your dining room accommodate a bar cart in the corner; does the study also have space for a sofa bed? Keep in mind power points (or lack thereof): if placing the TV in one particular alcove means training extension leads across a fireplace, you might need to rethink, or hire an electrician.

See also page 80: My space is too big!

Above: A brand new extension gives you free rein to turn it into whatever you like (if it's not already earmarked as a kitchen or bathroom). By cleverly incorporating bookshelves around the glazing area, this relatively modest room can incorporate both a dining table and seating nook.

Below: Make the most of the chance to buy furniture items to best fit your new space. Modular pieces, like this corner sofa, could allow you to create something semi-bespoke that you can add to or reconfigure later as needed.

SPLASHING THE CASH: Where to invest and where to save

Some people seem to have a knack for creating a stylish living space for very little outlay, while others can invest thousands and still not quite get it right. Here's how you could save a few bob on five key features and get a great look on the cheap.

1. Soft seating
A bold, bright sofa – whether patterned or plain – offers a real talking point, but can be a daunting purchase. If you're feeling nervous, test the water with a statement armchair in a vibrant hue and save a little cash.

2. Fancy furniture
When it comes to tabletop materials of choice, nothing much tops marble (both in looks *and* in price). If you're eyeing up a piece of furniture made from lower-quality materials, consider its shape over anything else: something with good bones can scrub up brilliantly with a lick of paint, or you could even go faux and apply marble-effect contact paper to the top.

3. Statement wallpaper
All-over patterned papers have made a comeback in recent years, and they are certainly striking. If your budget is stretched, wallpapering only a limited area might mean that you can afford a design that would otherwise be prohibitively expensive.

4. Industrial lighting
Bare bulbs continue to be hot in interiors, both aesthetically and literally. A pendant with a strong silhouette can really make a space, but the humble vintage-flex-and-bare-bulb combination is a classic option that can be installed at little cost and offers flexibility.

5. Fixtures and fittings
Scrimping on taps can be a false economy, so instead of buying cheap versions of on-trend industrial designs, get a little creative and befriend a plumber. They may be able to make you something bespoke for very little outlay, for instance by using copper pipes and no-nonsense garden taps.

1

How can I highlight the period details in my home?

In brief: Use colour and careful refurbishment to flatter what you have, explore ways to replace what's been lost, or nod to the past in unexpected, modern ways

Period details: if you've got 'em, flaunt 'em, and if you haven't, you can always fashion a workaround. Whether your house was built in the 1860s or the 1960s, chances are it has at least some original features still intact, even if they're hidden behind plasterboard or under carpet, so dig around a bit and see what you can unearth. Whatever your interiors style, such details are almost always to be celebrated: elaborate Victorian cornicing can create a wonderful juxtaposition with an otherwise modern interior, while Mid-Century retro fixtures and fittings have a warm, comforting appeal.

Creating colour contrasts is one way to highlight such features. You can flag up ornate skirting boards and dado rails with different tones, or even paint a ceiling in a dark or vibrant hue to showcase a stunning ceiling rose. Conversely, a popular contemporary approach is to paint both walls and details – from skirting boards to window frames – in the same matt tone throughout. If delicate details or beautiful old materials have been dulled or damaged under decades of paint, invest the time and effort in stripping them back with an appropriate chemical paint remover or heat gun. Finally, celebrate any imperfections – you can even leave them unpainted – to reveal your home's heritage, warts and all, and heighten the contrast with the rest of your scheme.

If you are considering adding missing period details to your house once more, do your research and aim to install pieces that are appropriate to the age of the property. Adding fussy Victorian detailing to a bland modern building, for example, will only create a pastiche. That's not to say that you can't have a little fun, though: try installing a group of old ceiling roses as alternative wall decor for a quirky touch, or place old carved picture mouldings above contemporary door frames. Wooden panelling, such as tongue-and-groove or wainscoting, can be easy to fake using new timber, embellished with wood beading trim or mouldings if required; simply paint over them with chalk paint and they will instantly take on a timeless quality.

See also page 76: I love the industrial warehouse style …
but I live in a suburban semi

Above left: Treating both walls and woodwork in the same tone gives a contemporary feel, instantly modernizing any Lincrusta-style embossed wallpapers or fussy woodwork detailing, and leaving the eye free to take in the various details of the space as it passes over them, without distraction.

Above right: Placing pared-back, modern pieces in bold hues within an otherwise ornate room provides a charming juxtaposition between the fussy and the fun. If the space were filled with traditional furnishings, the overall effect would feel very different.

Below: The bold patterned wall adds an unexpected modern hit amid the surrounding traditional wainscoting, instantly transforming this from a purely period space to more of a fusion of styles and eras.

Tip

Paint applied to woodwork in the 1970s or earlier may contain lead (telltale signs include a flaky, 'scaly' appearance). You can buy inexpensive lead paint testing kits online - if lead is found, take precautions when sanding or stripping the affected area by fully covering all surrounding surfaces, wearing protective clothing and wetting all surfaces before you start any work.

How can I stop our family living space from feeling like a crèche?

In brief: Invest in grown-up storage solutions and make it easy to clear things away, ensuring that any larger pieces that have to remain on show relate to your interior

It's an unfortunate truth that kids mean clutter, and usually lots of it. Even if you're lucky enough to have a dedicated playroom, it's inevitable that Lego bricks and Barbie dolls will infiltrate grown-up areas, especially if your living room has to do double duty as a children's jungle gym. The key to a space that doesn't stifle creative play yet is easy to 're-adult' when required is to create ways of tidying things up as quickly and easily as possible, while minimizing the glaring 'kiddiness' of what's left.

Children's storage is typically less than attractive, and although it's great for encouraging them to tidy their bedrooms, there's no real benefit to choosing lurid, cartoon-emblazoned toy boxes in your main living space. Consider ways of storing things so that children can still access them easily and – crucially – put them away afterwards. Colourful woven baskets can be used to separate different types of toy, and a large ottoman will work just as well as a toy box, and also double up as extra seating. Encourage your children to take ownership of their stuff (or trick them into tidying under the guise of 'playing grown-ups') by getting them to handwrite labels for storage boxes or bins, and give them the challenge of putting things back in the right place. Make the most of walls by installing chunky low-level hooks that you can use to hang oversized bags holding soft toys or fancy-dress outfits, and play mats that cinch up into storage bags for small items such as wooden or plastic bricks. Conversely, a higher peg rail will house items that you want to keep out of the reach of tiny hands. Create defined areas for play, such as a mini reading nook or a little painting table tucked into a corner.

Bear in mind the appearance of oversized pieces such as ride-on trikes or train sets, and allow yourself to consider your own taste as well as the educational and developmental benefits of each piece. Choosing toys and other pieces made from wood and natural materials over plastic is better not only for the environment but also for aesthetics. Since it's inevitable that toys will sometimes be left out (OK, most of the time), at least if they're not too offensive it should be a little more bearable.

Above: Woven storage baskets like these would be relatively easy to recreate at home by adding some custom labelling onto a plain basket with a yarn needle and some coloured wool. Draw on your design first with pencil, then use a backstitch to cover over it with thread.

Below left: An upright crate tucked into a corner next to a beanbag makes for a cute, versatile reading nook for quiet times – books can be housed both in and on the crate. Opting for a sweet yet simple design on the beanbag, like this star print, will appeal to kids and adults alike.

Below right: You can still incorporate bright primary tones into a space without it feeling overwhelmingly kiddie – just keep it to smaller pops, like this bunting, and temper with plenty of white or neutral tones.

What are the best window treatments for a tricky area?

In brief: Use curtains and blinds to disguise the ugly or highlight the lovely, through strategic hanging and positioning

Some architects would prefer us all to live in glass boxes overlooking views of nature, without anything as trivial or distracting as curtains to sully their structures, but for most people and most rooms, a window treatment of some description is essential for managing light, privacy and cosiness. The average rectangular window won't cause too many problems – mount a curtain rail or track above it, or fix shutters or a blind into the recess – but some can be much trickier to dress.

Think about your style preference before working out if your window can accommodate it. If you love cosy, sweeping curtains but the window goes right up to the ceiling, could you fit a ceiling-mounted track, or realistically would a blind made from a sumptuous fabric work better? If you covet the clean lines of shutters but can't fit them into the window recess, would a chunky slatted blind fitted outside the window frame give you the look you want? Unusually shaped windows, for instance ones with a semicircular top, deserve to be left on show, so try to fix window treatments that stay well clear when open. For less-than-lovely windows, on the other hand – particularly if they're small, oddly shaped or simply a mishmash – it may be best if you almost ignore them. A stunning wall of floor-length curtains that you can pull across the whole lot will look a lot more considered than several smaller treatments (use sheer fabric if you want to keep them drawn during the day).

To elongate a stubby window visually (and to maximize the available light), hang a Roman blind as high above the top of the window as you can without exposing the top of the frame. This will trick the eye into thinking the window is taller than it really is. For a very narrow window, adapt the same trick with wide curtains mounted either side. Tension rods can be useful for dormer windows or others where the glazing takes up the entire wall, allowing you to fit it between the two facing walls. For a more casual (or even temporary) approach, tie string or ribbon from fixings at the top of the window and suspend lightweight fabric, held in place with curtain clips.

Above left: The clean lines of this industrial-modern space are well suited to Venetian blinds like these. Cleanly fitting into the recess, they offer adjustability, yet all but disappear when left fully open.

Above right: Some simple voile fabric can be relatively inexpensive yet look surprisingly luxe when treated generously. If your window is a funny shape or in an awkward spot, allow it to cascade floor to ceiling and right across the wall where the window is situated, for a diffused glow and hotel-chic vibe.

Below: A simple, extra-wide curtain track leaves the striking curved top of this statement window totally unobscured when the curtains are open, allowing them ample space to hang either side without hiding anything. Tailoring the curtains so the drop is the exact height of the windowsill ensures they won't crumple at the bottom when drawn.

Tip

The general rule for hanging curtains is to place your pole or track around 15cm/6" higher than the top of your window frame, and around 15–20cm/ 6–8" wider at either side. Curtains themselves should be between 1.5–2 times the width of the window, depending on how generous you want the pleats, and hung on or just under the windowsill, or left at floor length. For blinds that are being fitted outside of the window recess, add on an extra 10cm/4" to both width and length, to ensure they fully cover the window.

I want my bathroom to feel like a luxury spa

In brief: Introduce calm with zen lighting, sleek storage and a few stand-out statements

The bathrooms we encounter in boutique hotels and spas are generally dedicated to pampering and decadent downtime, unlike the typical home bathroom, which can be a chaotic space where we try to shave and brush our teeth at the same time while attempting to ignore ever-worsening cracks in the grouting. Bringing a touch of the former to the latter can have a real impact on the way the room looks and feels, and can even help to improve our overall well-being.

A show-stopping roll-top bath can be the ultimate luxury item in a bathroom, but it needn't be too expensive or take up much more space than a standard tub if you shop around for budget or compact designs. Floor-standing or wall-mounted taps increase the sense of decadence. In fact, whatever your tub, it can be wise to chase pipes into walls anywhere you can, to allow for wall-mounted fixtures and fittings. This contributes to a streamlined look and leaves fewer places for mould to build up. In fact, unsexy though it may be, hygiene and ease of cleaning are crucial to making a bathroom feel luxurious, so streamline sanitaryware and accessories as much as possible and ensure a high-quality finish throughout, so that you can wipe up quickly when you need to restore order.

Add extra zen by layering lighting, perhaps installing it on a dimmer switch or with separate switches for each light source; you could even consider chromotherapy mood lighting in your bath or shower area, to aid relaxation. A rainfall shower head can be invigorating and immersive. And be sure to include built-in recesses or slim shelving to house scented candles and favourite toiletries, so they don't clutter up the edges of the bath or shower tray. When it comes to decor, a simple, timeless look often works best, so stick to a restricted palette of warm, gentle patterns and colours, bringing in texture with fluffy towels and a ruglike bathmat. Storage is also key to success: one of the reasons that boutique hotel bathrooms look so chic is that they're not housing a family pack of toilet rolls and a selection of cleaning sprays, so keep all those ugly but necessary items strictly behind closed doors.

See also page 78: How do I bring light into my windowless bathroom?

Rolling up towels neatly, rather than just shoving roughly folded ones onto a shelf, can instantly evoke hotel chic at no cost. Avoid letting ugly plastic bottles sully things by decanting everyday items like shampoo or hand wash into sleek dispensers, or splash out on a set of posh products with fancy packaging, then when they run out just top them up with cheaper lotions and potions.

I've chosen a neutral scheme – how can I jazz it up without resorting to colour?

In brief: Mix various warm off-whites with textural furnishings, accents and accessories, incorporating lots of natural materials

Neutral certainly needn't mean bland, if it's handled right, and there are a myriad ways to add interest and personality through other means if vibrant hues aren't your thing. A neutral scheme is nothing to be sniffed at: indeed, it can create a relaxing, calming sanctuary that can work particularly well in a study or bedroom that you want to be free of distraction. The first thing to bear in mind is the base. Simply sloshing bright white emulsion over everything won't create the best backdrop, and in fact it can make the space feel cold. Mixing complementary neutral shades will give you the softest result: perhaps pale taupe walls with a hint of blush on ceilings and woodwork, or a pale French grey punctuated with crisp ivory.

It's crucial to incorporate varied textures and materials in a neutral space. Natural materials exude warmth, even if said material is a pale marble rather than a rustic oak. Bringing in warm wood, stone and metal and mixing them with tactile, easy-living materials such as linen, sheepskin and felt will add that all-important three-dimensional quality. Most eco-friendly finishes have a natural, flawed tactility that is perfect for a neutral scheme. A swathe of retro materials has recently come firmly back into fashion for these very reasons, including cork flooring, woven rattan seats and bamboo side tables. Houseplants – that other retro revival – also lift a neutral scheme wonderfully, breathing life into it without overpowering the pale-and-interesting theme.

The great thing about neutrals is that they all tend to go together effortlessly, making them a relatively easy choice. But if you want to add punch, use accents of dark grey, bitter chocolate or even warm black to break things up without introducing an actual colour. Such hues work well for woodwork, within wall art (black-and-white photography always looks timeless), or as part of a pattern in flooring or rugs. They can also be incorporated into a subtle wallpaper print or used as a dark stain on light-painted wood, to give a dirty, distressed contrast.

Above: By painting it dark, in contrast with this otherwise light space, the beautiful bay window is allowed to become the star of the show. Clever uses of dark tones throughout the rest of the room, from the daybed to the inside of the fireplace, ensure the contrast is balanced rather than jarring.

Below left: Sticking to subtle patterns and a pale or grey colourway means areas of wallpaper can be brought in without it feeling overwhelming. By keeping it contained and bringing the same tones into the rest of the space, the look is still very easy on the eye.

Below right: A collection of mismatched mirrors is united by the frames, all painted in the same dark tone, which marry in with the floor tiles, both in shape and colour. Although adding little in the way of pattern, they still manage to make a real statement on the walls.

Is the feature wall a cliché?

In brief: Not necessarily – but there are ways of stopping it from feeling half-baked

It felt as if the world reached Peak Feature Wall several years ago, as we all fell over ourselves to turn our chimney breasts into statement centrepieces. The interiors world has kicked back since then, and as we grow bolder, and find ourselves staying in our homes for longer rather than climbing up the property ladder, there has been a rise in homeowners choosing (gasp) to wallpaper entire rooms, leaving the painted or papered single feature looking rather old hat.

It's by no means over for the feature wall, but it must be handled appropriately or it will feel dated. One mistake many decorators make is to slap a vibrant hue or bold pattern on to one area without understanding its impact, rather than harnessing it as a tool to improve the visual flow of the whole space. It's very common to enhance the prominence of a chimney breast in this way, but, rather than make it more elegant, this can simply cause it to stick out like a sore thumb, particularly if the surrounding walls are left in a safe neutral that bears no relation to the brighter colour. It's often better to use your statement colour or paper inside the alcoves on either side; not only will this look subtler overall (but no less striking), but if you choose a darker tone or pattern, it will create the illusion that the walls are receding, enhancing the feeling of space. Likewise, adding dark patterns and colours to the end walls of a long, narrow room can help it to appear less tunnel-like. In a bedroom, where a busy all-over pattern might not be conducive to relaxation, a bold design behind the bedhead will add impact without distracting you when you're trying to sleep.

Using colour and pattern to punctuate certain spaces can be useful in a large or multifunctional room, visually 'claiming' the different zones, but carry the colour through into accent pieces to stop it from feeling random. Of course, feature walls (or sections) needn't be limited to paint or paper: wooden cladding or patterned tiles would also do the job, for example. But if there's a nagging little voice inside you desperate to plaster that cool chevron print over all four walls, go for it: it'll only feel half-hearted if you don't.

A subtle, more nuanced pattern can be easier to blend into a space than anything too bold, and is a smart choice if you want a more refined look. From the curtains to the bedlinen, this room has been designed to ensure the feature wallpaper sits effortlessly within the overall scheme, rather than shouting for attention when you enter.

PAINT EFFECTS: Wow with your walls

Paint effects can add pattern and interest to walls while giving as much punch as wallpaper. Here are five ideas to whet your appetite.

1. Go geometric

Creating geometric patterns on your walls is immensely satisfying and surprisingly easy. Once you've decided on your colour palette, paint the wall in one overall shade, then use low-tack decorator's tape to add the pattern (plan it out first on paper, or freestyle it straight on to the wall). Work out which colours will go where, then paint them one colour at a time, allowing plenty of drying time between adjacent tones.

2. Opt for ombré

This requires a little more artistic finesse, but it's still possible for a DIYer. Start with three light, medium and darker versions of the same paint tone and paint the whole of your wall in the lightest tone. Leave to dry, then use a pencil to mark the wall lightly into three equal horizontal bands. Paint the middle and darkest colours on the middle and bottom sections respectively, then use a paint tray to make a 50:50 mix of the top and middle colours, and another to do the same with the middle and bottom colours. Use a dry, angled brush to work the appropriate colour mix quickly over the join between the top and middle band while the paint is still wet, dabbing with a damp sponge to rework certain areas as you go if the paint dries before you're happy. Repeat on the lower half with your other colour mix.

3. Jagged lines

A bold tone on the bottom third of a paler wall is a striking way to add a feature colour. Rather than separating the two tones with a straight line, however, play about and create something more interesting. Draw a straight pencil line across the wall where you want the bold colour to end, and paint roughly up to it, then remove most of the paint from your brush and pull it upwards at an angle, working systematically along the wall.

4. Watered-down wash

Start with a clean, sound wall painted white (or light), then decant your chosen colour and some decorator's glaze into a paint kettle and mix (patch test in an inconspicuous spot until you're happy with the consistency; you might prefer to water the paint down first). Apply it lightly to the wall using an extra-wide soft paintbrush and long, irregular strokes, so that you can see the brush marks and the wall colour beneath. If you'd rather not see brushstrokes, work over the wall immediately with a lint-free cloth to 'rub' in the colour gently.

5. Accent colour block

A colour block in an unexpected place can be striking. As with the geometric wall, paint the wall with the base colour first, then use decorator's tape to block out where the accent will go. To get a crisp, pristine line, paint over the inner edges of the tape with the main colour and leave to dry before painting on the accent colour. When you remove the tape, there will be no colour-bleeding.

1

How can I create a gallery-style art display without making a mess?

In brief: Follow one (but not all) of the curation rules to create your perfect arrangement, and consider alternative wall fixings to minimize damage

Pinterest makes the picture wall look effortless, especially when the image you're admiring appears to be a mishmash of styles with no discernible scheme to speak of, yet still looks oh-so-perfect. But first impressions can be deceptive, and – as with so many things – there's an art to getting it right, despite the impression of chaos. There are some basic rules; the trick is choosing which to follow.

When it comes to curating, the best rule of thumb is to work out which 'rule' you're going to follow in the first place, and stick to it. The most common plans of attack are to link your display via theme (say, all botanical prints or figurative drawings), colour/s (regardless of subject), frame type (everything in simple black frames, for example, or even all unframed canvases) and configuration (such as everything fitting neatly into an 'invisible' grid to create a rectangular shape overall, or an arrangement with an uneven outer shape but equal spacing between all the objects within it). It can help to lay the pieces out on the floor before committing them to the walls, so that you can play with them to create the most pleasing arrangement, or you can even cut out pieces of newspaper the same size as your prints and tape them to the walls, to give you a feel for the position of everything.

In terms of quite literally not making a mess, there are ways to hang several prints without littering the wall with pockmarks. The good thing about choosing to display many small artworks rather than one or two large ones is that they are much lighter, and therefore less likely to require you to butcher your walls with clunky screw holes. For some framed prints, a slim picture pin might offer adequate support, or for unframed ones, fixing them in place with washi tape could be an option (and will bring a contemporary, casual air to the arrangement). It's worth looking at removable sticky fixing pads and hooks designed specifically not to damage walls – perfect for renters and the indecisive alike. Alternatively, install a picture ledge: it's a one-time-only hole-making affair, and then you can rearrange its contents over the years to your heart's content without marking the walls.

Above left: This display of prints and framed foliage doesn't follow any firm rules, but still looks stunning thanks to its artful curation and dramatic setting. Despite going a little off-piste, the display does follow a nature-inspired theme and the muted palette makes it easy on the eye.

Above right: This eclectic mix of art and ephemera looks clean rather than cluttered thanks to its strict rectangular arrangement. Utilizing unusual shapes, like a small pennant flag, adds interest.

Below: A picture ledge offers freedom to change arrangements at whim, and adds a somewhat informal look to a space. It can be a good option for anything that might otherwise be tricky to hang – a colourful vintage tile, say, or a beautiful old book cover.

I live in a new-build – how can I add character?

In brief: Use reclaimed materials and furniture from different eras to inject soul, juxtaposing them with their modern surroundings for a warm, layered appearance

Owners of period properties with original features have a head start when it comes to decorating, with a fireplace that already demands to be the focal point of the room, or original Victorian tiling that naturally dictates the colour scheme. So it's easy to feel overwhelmed when you're confronted instead with a sterile beige box, with little to help you distinguish between the rooms, or even the floors. Seek ways of creating your own focal points, instead, and add a careful balance of pieces in various styles and from different periods, to create the depth and soul that are missing.

An ostentatious marble fireplace in a one-bedroom flat built in 1993 is not the most sympathetic addition, but creating a focal point that isn't the TV can make a living space more rounded in design terms. A no-nonsense wood-burning stove will work a treat (or an electric equivalent, if installation of the necessary flue would be prohibitive), or use a striking sideboard or console table in the most prominent place, styled with your favourite vases or other objects. Bringing in reclaimed materials adds soul instantly – cladding a wall with characterful old timbers, for example, or using reclaimed encaustic tiles to cover a kitchen floor and provide a charming contrast with contemporary units. You can get the same effect with vintage furniture: a dining table with a roughed-up lime-washed top will instantly add personality, or try placing a charming wingback armchair to one side of a modern sofa.

Your space will presumably have come with all walls painted a tasteful, inoffensive shade of bland, so breaking things up with a new scheme, or even just a few tonal hues thrown in here and there, will help to give each room its own identity. Choosing heritage hues with a flat matt finish can help to lessen the 'newness' of everything more than vibrant, contemporary shades might. Texture, too, will instantly add interest: try throwing down a few chunky woven rugs over that beige carpet or cheap laminate, or even ripping up the flooring and going with the bare concrete or utilitarian wood sub-floor, for an industrial twist.

See also page 76: I love the industrial warehouse style …
but I live in a suburban semi

Above: The owners of this new-build flat opted to simply paint their MDF sub-flooring, rather than installing costly laminate. By sanding, prepping with an MDF primer, then painting with hardwearing floor paint, they've achieved an original yet contemporary feel. Gentle vintage elements, such as the angled wall lamp and Ercol coffee table, give a nuanced look.

Below left: In order to blend this new kitchen extension in with the rest of the Victorian property, reclaimed scaffold boards, crackled 'imperfect' handmade brick tiles and vintage-style cup handles were all used to allude to period charm and ensure the addition didn't jar with the rest of the house.

Below right: Painted grey or dark metal sliding or bi-fold doors can look a lot more considered than standard white. The mix of different vintage furniture and the coastal-inspired light fitting give this space a laid-back, casual air.

Tip

If your home really is brand spanking new, leave the walls alone for at least six months before repainting or hanging wallpaper, to give the plaster a chance to settle.

How do I arrange my ornaments to look curated?

In brief: Three really *is* the magic number (although five or seven also work well). Play with scale and group odd numbers of trinkets, using trays or tablecloths to ground them

While ornaments may be instrumental in helping a house feel like a home, they can simply feel like clutter if they're not handled with care. A solitary line-up of unrelated (or even perfectly coordinated) pieces can feel sad and spartan, so think in terms of three-dimensional curations rather than simply running things along a few edges. A symmetrical scheme can be restful for the eye, but requires careful configuration and can feel staged, so it's better to work with odd numbers and varying heights. Our brains respond naturally to arrangements that obey these rules, forcing our eyes to move up, along and around in order to take everything in, so such groupings are – unsurprisingly – more visually interesting.

As well as bearing in mind the Rule of Odds, make sure that there's enough space between the groupings, so the eye is not overwhelmed. Working with vignettes of objects from a similar 'family' – whether quite literally multiples of single items (a cluster of pillar candles, say) or more casual acquaintances (such as a collection of otherwise unrelated trinkets all made from natural materials) – can be a good approach to begin with. A difference in silhouette is paramount for this, so consider the shape of the pieces as well. With a set of vases, for instance, a mixture of geometric, curved and rounded shapes will have more impact than a group with similar proportions. Introducing smaller, subtler pieces can help things to feel fuller, and they won't vie for attention with your primary display pieces.

This rule can also be applied to wall-hanging objects, such as artwork. A painting or print hung off-centre a little way above your arrangement can ground the grouping. Consider practical elements, too: books stacked on a coffee table, or a bedside display that incorporates a lamp, plant, alarm clock, mug and pretty tube of hand cream. Finally, though, don't feel obliged to adhere so rigidly to any of the above that you're forced to discard much-loved items: above all else, if it makes you happy, roll with it.

See also page 64: I'm a collector – how can I best display my prized possessions?

Above left: Trays can be a useful and practical addition to a tabletop arrangement: use them to visually anchor flowers or trinkets, then if you need to clear a little space for something more important like, um, a cake, it's easy to lift it all off in one go.

Above right: This fun, poppy colour palette is bold but not overwhelming, thanks to mixing some neutral and pastel shades among the brights.

Below: Vintage paperback books not only look lovely, they can also make for a useful styling prop, helping to add height to an arrangement and break things up somewhat. The odd unusually shaped *objet*, such as an animal ornament, can add some extra interest and a touch of personality.

What can I do with my unused fireplace?

In brief: Treat it as a styling opportunity, creating interesting arrangements in the empty space, or use the 'cover or distract' approach

A period fireplace can be a thing of great charm, yet also something of an eyesore if it has been crudely part-removed, boxed in or 'modernized'. If your room has a fireplace that doesn't function (and if reinstating its working bits isn't on the cards), see it as a styling opportunity to have a little fun and inject some personality.

If you've just been left with a hole, you could choose function-appropriate props and fill it with decorative cut logs, a selection of pillar candles (or LED versions) or simply a string of fairy lights to give a little twinkle. You could even add an iron fire basket and some artfully charred kindling for convincing fakery. If you'd prefer to be a little more adventurous, fill the gap with shade-loving plants such as a delicate asparagus fern, or with striking faux flowers, or use it as a miniature stage to create a display of succulents or seashells. A larger spot, such as an inglenook, could almost be treated as a tiny room, and you could place a floor cushion and a crate of books in there to create a little snug.

If you haven't been left with an elegantly blackened brick interior, decorate the fireplace by tiling the hole with a statement patterned tile (a gloss finish will help to bounce light around). A shelf fixed above it could offer more impact, acting as a makeshift mantel. Many ugly surrounds can be transformed with a lick of paint; in fact, you might be surprised how readily paint can turn a retro crazy-paved monstrosity into something just the right side of Mid-Century chic, or how a garish orange 1980s brick surround can become altogether more subtle with the application of watered-down chalk paint.

The best approach for the sad boxed-in fireplace, where unforgiving boarding hides the place where its fiery heart once roared, is to hide its shortcomings in plain sight. Add an eye-catching graphic design across the covering with paint, wallpaper or fabric, place a decorative fire screen or large artwork in front of it, or group bushy pot plants to disguise it, and hope no one notices.

Placing plants on raised boxes (a solid old suitcase or upturned fruit crate would also work) creates a podium for them, as well as hiding some of the (missing) internal fireplace fittings. As larger pot plants are generally more expensive, it could be a cost-effective option, too, boosting the height of a smaller specimen.

My home is in permanent shade

In brief: Use metallic, glossy or reflective surfaces to bounce around the light you do have, and be clever with mirrors

A room that is naturally gloomy can be a real turn-off. Whether the cause is small windows, orientation or shadows cast from outside (the last two being pretty much impossible to rectify), the tricks to make things feel lighter and brighter are the same. If you *are* able to get the sledgehammer out, it's wise to consult an architect first to determine what will maximize the light coming in, whether that be adding a glass-box extension, swapping a standard window for a floor-to-ceiling one or even putting in internal glazed windows or doors, to borrow light from elsewhere.

For now, let's assume you're in need of some tricks. In essence, this means bouncing around what light you do have. So for walls and trims, options include painting them with satin paint or even a subtle, shimmery emulsion (look out for specialist 'feature wall' paints), going over woodwork in a high-gloss finish or using wallpaper with metallic or reflective qualities. Furniture could also be given the glossy paint treatment, or choose mirrored pieces, or ones made from glass or acrylic for their high sheen. For soft furnishings and accessories, materials with a natural sheen will help: think silk throws, fabrics with metallic woven threads for cushions and curtains, deep-pile carpeting (or rugs) and velvet-upholstered furniture. Mirrors can also be very helpful in a dingy room. Place a floor-standing one between two windows to trick the eye into seeing the area as one large light source; put one opposite a window to reflect the limited light coming in; or even use a large sheet of mirror to line an alcove. If your budget is tight, make a feature wall of several small mirrors that you can add to over time, to give a relaxed, eclectic look.

Add illumination creatively by using lampshades with reflective interiors and accessories with a foxed-silver finish, for example. Make sure you don't inadvertently introduce elements that might suck out the light, such as dark artworks that will absorb light, or heavy curtains that get in the way of the precious illumination that *is* available.

See also page 70: How do I tackle my north-facing room?

With its reflective properties, this wallpaper helps the light move throughout the space; as the pattern and background are both pale, they don't offer too much distraction to the eye. Stick to light furniture and accessories in similar colours to prevent anything from feeling gloomy.

We're setting up house together: how do we combine our styles (and stuff)?

In brief: Seek out common ground, be it a few shared colours or materials, and try to balance scale and repetition while embracing the mismatched

Whether moving in with a new beau or starting up a house-share, most of us come with some sort of (physical) baggage, from the odd pot plant to a full suite of furniture. Successfully blending it all can have as much to do with diplomatic relations as with design ideals, but fortunately schemes involving mixed styles and tastes can be very successful, so take it as an opportunity to create an environment with lots of personality.

If you're sharing or lodging, it makes sense to restrict more outlandish schemes to your own bedroom, so concentrate on getting that to your taste first, to give you an idea of the best approach for communal spots. Otherwise, simply start with the room that needs the most urgent attention, or that you'll be using the most. While accommodating others' tastes is the best way to create harmony among cohabitees, don't compromise to the point of creating something 'vanilla' that doesn't please anyone. If one of you is more creative, consider appointing that person primary 'designer', especially in a multi-person house-share, to avoid too many vying opinions.

When mixing styles, the key to prevent things from looking like a jumble is to let one element take the lead. If you're mixing contemporary pieces with chintzy Victoriana, for example, strip back one style and ensure it becomes more an accent than the main event. Seek out features that unite rather than divide: when things aren't matching in the traditional sense, is there something else that can pull them together, such as a few prominent colours? Do the legs of your sofa happen to match the wooden top of your flatmate's coffee table, and could you extend that to a third object? Mirroring can also work, so placing two different side tables either side of a sofa, for example, will give a modicum of symmetry even if they don't actually match. Try to mix the different styles evenly throughout the room and treat it as a whole, rather than having 'your' items dress one set of shelves and your housemate's on a sideboard. If you're in the market for buying extras, choose pieces that bridge any gaps, like an armchair that picks out a key colour, or a decorative object that sits somewhere between the dominant styles.

Despite the different styles and eras, these country-style chairs marry perfectly with the retro table thanks to their shared glossy white coating. If you prefer a modicum of matchy-matchy, painting disparate pieces to match can be a clever way to tie everything together, especially when things come from different sources.

'I'M NOT CREATIVE': Unleash your inner designer step by step

If design doesn't come naturally to you, pretend to be your own client: work out your needs, wants and likes and create a blueprint for implementing your dream scheme.

1. Pull together visuals
They needn't be fancy – just compile tear sheets from magazines, pull out some favourite photos and add anything else that you like the look of, then cast a critical eye over the whole lot and work out what it is you actually like overall. Is it a particular colour or specific design detail, or is it the general mood? What can you learn from this, and what could you actually apply to your room?

2. Choose your design direction
Avoid getting too hung up on following a particular theme, or your room risks feeling staged. Think instead about the kind of overall look that might work for you, based on the previous step, while taking into account existing furnishings or decor and how your ideas might work with your specific property. This could involve a few general styles – modern retro, say, or rustic Scandi.

3. Work out a colour palette
Pick out the key colours from your favourite images in Step 1, and consider how they fit into your design direction and how you might use them. If in doubt, narrow it down to three main tones and aim to use them in different quantities: your primary colour overall; a secondary tone for about one-third; and any bolder hues as an accent only. Consider the light entering the space, whether it's cool or warm, bright or diffused, and adapt your choices accordingly.

4. Source your key or statement pieces
This is usually the most dominant piece of furniture, such as the sofa in a living room or the table in a dining space, but if you've set your heart on a bold wallpaper or show-stopping light fitting, build out from

that instead. With investment pieces, use a modicum of restraint to make sure that you have a relatively classic basis on which to layer more trend-led pieces. If you're creating a jewel-inspired scheme, for example, a plain Chesterfield with colourful buttons might be a wiser option than a sofa covered in patterned upholstery.

5. Finesse with finishing touches
Now you can start thinking about layering in those all-important pieces that play a supporting role in making your space come to life: soft furnishings, decorative accessories, lighting, rugs and wall art are all key to creating a polished finish. These finishing pieces can easily be picked up for peanuts with a bit of savvy shopping or creative upcycling, which is just as well, since this is usually the point when the budget seems to evaporate. Give things a lift by mixing pieces from different periods, or incorporating the odd vintage item, regardless of your scheme.

1

2

3

X

4

5

I have no entryway

In brief: Create a feeling of separation with strategically placed furniture and clever flooring, or embrace the boundary-less vibe and simply ensure that you have good storage for outdoor detritus

Walking directly into a living area from the street can sometimes feel … well, icky, for want of a better word. But when space is limited, or all internal walls have been removed in a quest for open-plan zen, sometimes we've just got to live with it. Returning a sense of definition will help things to feel slightly less in-your-face and provide an opportunity to keep outdoor detritus concealed from view; there are various ways of achieving this without calling in the builders.

You can create a semi-partition 'wall' by placing a bookcase or shelving unit perpendicular to the door wall; such pieces can do double duty by storing coats and shoes, too. If that's likely to cut out valuable light, choose an open-sided unit and place more decorative pieces on it, instead. Alternatively, try to create a defined hallway area by fixing up a few wall hooks and placing a bench underneath that could house footwear as well as visually anchoring the spot. A floor runner leading directly away from the door will give definition, or even use different flooring just in that area to create the effect of a corridor, without the boundaries. A few carefully placed plants could also be valuable. Use bulky pieces of furniture to create a natural walkway, such as placing a sofa so that you pass its back as you enter the space. This will have the added benefit of creating a more intimate sitting area.

Conversely, you may prefer to celebrate your lack of hallway by treating the whole area as one space, rather than trying to define it visually. This approach can create better flow and provide more circulation space in a restricted spot, but if you're not careful you can be left eyeballing your muddy dog-walking boots when you're trying to relax. Seek out hardworking, slimline storage to go along the wall by the door, so that you can tuck offending items out of sight. If your budget is tight, simple shelving with a curtain across the front is a cheaper way of creating something bespoke. And, speaking of curtains, if you're in a cool country and the front door leads directly outside, consider fitting one over the door (hanging it from portière rods is both practical and stylish) to stop draughts, as well as to hide the door.

Above: A half-height wall offers a degree of separation without losing light or space in this small open-plan area. Using a sideboard or console unit would do a similar job in a completely open hallway space.

Below left: Instead of seeking to visually separate the stairs from your living area, you could embrace it and treat the staircase as an architectural feature, using armchairs to give the space beneath a natural cosy look.

Below right: Storage is key to preventing an open hallway from feeling cluttered; reduce visual noise by keeping hooks and shelving the same colour as walls, for example. To stop things feeling messy, try to be ruthless about what's placed on shelves or hung up in this area.

I'm stuck with horrible textured wallpaper – what can I do to disguise it?

In brief: Don't despair: there are several options, from the superficial to the semi-permanent

Woodchip wallpaper: how did it ever seem like a good idea? This wallcovering nightmare (and its evil cousin, textured wallpaper), flung up so hastily to hide dodgy plasterwork from the 1960s onwards, now screams of cheap rental apartments. Even if you own your place, removing it can be a serious headache. It's still available to buy today, so someone, somewhere must still like it, but if it doesn't float your boat and you're not in a position to remove it, you'll probably be looking for ways to hide it.

First, if it's been painted in anything other than a flat matt emulsion, repaint it. The more matt the finish you use, the better, to minimize the light caught by those not-so-delightful dimples. Next, distract from it as much as you can. One way is simply to divert the eye by choosing, say, bold furniture or a heavily patterned rug. For the walls themselves, although it might seem counter-intuitive, making them busier with lots of artworks, particularly if you mix different shapes and styles, will draw the eye away from the surface itself. Another approach is to go big, by placing large wall hangings in strategic spots (behind sofas or bedheads can work well). A striking oversized macramé tapestry will offer a great distraction, or choose a piece of patterned fabric or even a pretty bedsheet. Think creatively – a cursory online search for 'party (or photography) backdrop ideas' will provide fun temporary or semi-permanent tricks to try. Solid objects can create the same effect: interesting old wooden shutters leaning against a wall, for instance, or an oversized vintage metal sign. Cladding a wall in wooden panelling or even pegboard is a more permanent solution that an enthusiastic DIYer could achieve.

For a more literal disguise, there are products that hide the lumps and bumps, such as specialist woodchip-covering wallpaper and substances that work a little like render, designed for the amateur decorator. But ultimately, if you need to rectify a large area, a wallpaper stripper and a lot of elbow grease might be the best bet after all.

See also page 104: How can I create a gallery-style art display without making a mess?

A custom hanging can cover a large swathe of wall in one hit. Take a length of dowel, tie some rope or twine to its ends (drill a hole in the dowel first then knot it through), then hang some decorative fabric, or even a lightweight rug, from the dowel, fixing it in place at the top with some stitches. A single drop of wallpaper could give the same effect – attach a couple of bulldog clips to the dowel and suspend it from those instead.

How can I make my small room feel bigger?

In brief: By tricking those peepers into thinking there's more to it than meets the eye

While small but perfectly formed is nothing to be ashamed of, many of us do aspire to inhabit larger spaces. Whether you want to embrace the cosy opportunities for *hygge* that a diminutive room can offer, or trick the eye into thinking the space is larger than it is, there's much that can be achieved, despite the limited proportions. Light colours are often recommended for small rooms, although darker hues can create a more intimate atmosphere; either way, keep to the same or similar tones on walls, ceilings and woodwork to avoid drawing attention to the boundaries of the room and to minimize distracting colour clashes. Anything that draws the eye upwards will increase the feeling of space, so install high, slim shelves close to the top of walls to house a collection of paperbacks, or hang vertically striped wallpaper (or horizontal stripes if you're after the illusion of width).

Designers will tell you to pull your furniture away from the walls to enhance the feeling of space. That's easier said than done when you live in a shoebox, but even angling the odd piece outwards can help the flow. Make sure your furniture works as hard as possible by making best use of the height of the room and choosing multi-purpose or hideaway items where possible, such as a storage coffee table or a wall-mounted drop-leaf table.

Rather than using small items of furniture, go for fewer pieces in larger dimensions; running generously proportioned rugs underneath legs will prevent your furniture from looking as though it's perched along the edges of the room. As with the walls, a stripy rug can look modern yet timeless and elongate the space – just don't have stripes on both walls and floor at the same time. Leggy furniture or semi-transparent accessories and fittings can aid the feeling of light and space and will be less obstructive than solid pieces; this goes for kitchens and bathrooms, too, where wall-hung base units or sanitaryware allow the eye to see right to the edges of the room. Be bold but restrained with accessories; by organizing them into cohesive, structured displays, you'll create attention-grabbing areas without overcrowding surfaces and making things look cluttered.

See also page 112: My home is in permanent shade

A limited colour palette used across two through-rooms helps unite the spaces as one, and confuses the eye as to where boundaries between spaces, floors and ceilings start and end. Opting for 'leggy' over chunky furniture allows the space to flow more freely, as does the choice of a single L-shaped sofa and slimline accent chair over a traditional three-piece suite.

My lighting feels stark – how can I soften it?

In brief: Layer it to accommodate the practical and the pleasing, just as you would with other elements of an interior

Nothing deadens a space quite like relying on a single ceiling light as the sole source of illumination. As an ambient light source (one that illuminates the space evenly) it is functionally important, but it can really kill the mood. Just as we might layer accent cushions and throws on our bed to make it feel inviting and cosy, so we should layer our lighting for the most pleasing effect. Take a moment to consider what you need and what you'd like. A directional task lamp by a corner chair is a necessity to prevent eye strain when reading, for example, whereas an accent light on a favourite artwork will add drama and a background glow while allowing you to appreciate the piece even more.

If you're specifically after softness, employ accent lighting in the form of uplighters. These can be freestanding or fixed, and can be worked into a scheme in many different ways. Providing a gentle wash of light, they give a relaxing glow along the top of a room, or add a subtle touch at ground level, by shining across the treads of stairs, for instance. Downlighters create more striking shadows. Your choice of bulb is important: warm (or even extra-warm) white light gives the softest glow, while LED filament bulbs offer a comforting, vintage-inspired aesthetic that's good enough to show off without a shade. Candles, string lights and even lit fires, while not necessarily bright enough to act as solo light sources, all add to the cosy, layered atmosphere.

In a naturally dark space, a daylight bulb (mimicking the make-up of natural light) can be helpful, particularly in a task lamp. Alternatively, a torchiere lamp directed at the ceiling in a particularly gloomy corner can be far less intrusive than putting on the main lights during a dull day. Consider, too, how you can customize the way you use your lighting: with dimmer switches on a circuit, you can fade and layer different lighting in different parts of the room, creating flexible lighting combinations. You could even do away with those pesky ceiling shades altogether and add dedicated sockets for lighting, so that you can switch free-standing lamps on and off at the wall.

Above left: Neon signs double up as artwork whether they are switched on or off, and offer a subtle atmospheric wash of lighting, often casting an interesting glow within the space they are situated in. Neon can be costly but its popularity has spawned a growing market in neon-effect flex, which offers a cheaper way to get the look.

Above right: String lights can work wonderfully to add a gentle glow to a corner. Micro lights on a clear flex are great for weaving across mirrors, around headboards or along shelving; or for a more retro statement, choose a string of chunky festoon lighting.

Below: A mixture of lighting types is imperative in a dark space. Here, drum shades on bedside lamps cast a warm wash of both uplight and downlight, while a table lamp across the room provides practical illumination by a mirror. A supersized chandelier adds a sense of grandeur and luxe as well as providing a general glow.

How do I combine different tones of wooden furniture?

In brief: Ensure there is a common tonality between the various woods, embrace and highlight their differences and use other elements to break things up

Natural wood has an almost indescribable charm, and generally becomes better-looking with age. Yet, without balance, it can feel overpowering, particularly when we find ourselves with different types of wood, or too much of it (floorboards, plus wall cladding, plus Granny's old teak dining table for good measure). If you're not sure whether you've reached wood overkill, take a moment to assess: is there something in the space that jars with everything else and, if so, could you move it elsewhere or paint it? Often, what works or doesn't work will come down to the undertone of the wood, rather than the style of the furniture itself. Warm woods containing red, orange or yellow undertones, such as walnut and maple, will work together well for a more classic look, while cooler, blonde woods with a grey-tinged cast can lend themselves to cool, contemporary Scandi-inspired styles.

When old and new woods are cleverly juxtaposed, the unique patina of the former can stand out beautifully from the latter: by teaming a weatherworn reclaimed-wood tabletop with a slick, modern engineered-wood floor, for example. Similarly, incorporating different finishes – say, a high-gloss cherry-veneer cabinet with an accent piece in rustic elm – can highlight the charms of each finish while remaining within the same colour family.

Use the undertone of your dominant wood to guide your paint colours, whether for other furniture you plan to paint, or for the walls themselves. Warm neutrals such as putty or bone white will quietly flatter warm woods, and a yellow-based green provides a harmonious backdrop for honey-toned woods such as pine. In a scheme where wood is dominant, it can help to pull everything together if you keep other elements fairly tight, for instance by limiting other colours or patterns while ensuring that they are repeated throughout, for unity. Don't forget to accessorize and accentuate with other materials. Warm metals flatter warm wood beautifully, while rough concrete can be just the right hue when teamed with pale, pinkish oak. If in doubt, consider painting one wooden element out altogether, like the floorboards, or for an easier option just break up the direct contact by placing a rug between floor and furniture.

Despite the dominance of wood - from the walls and floors to the kitchen units and tabletop - this charming living space manages to feel light and airy thanks to the clever use of stark white chairs to break things up, along with light walls and upper cabinetry in the kitchen. The wooden wall, kitchen units and tabletop share a warm rustic flavour, while the wood of the floor is pale enough to blend into the background, allowing the other elements to shine.

Is it possible to create a tasteful children's room?

In brief: Absolutely, if you avoid gender clichés and gimmicks

Kids' rooms can be a place where you can really let your (I mean, their) hair down and have a little fun with the design, so, rather than writing them off as taste-free zones destined to feature only dog-eared posters of boy bands and naff tractor or princess motifs, embrace the bold, fun patterns and hues they can take and allow everyone's imagination to run wild. Making the space broadly gender-neutral is a practical way of accommodating ever-changing little tastes, as well as giving them an unrestricted space where they can play as they please.

As is so often the case with design, if you're after something clean and contemporary yet effortlessly chic, be inspired by Scandinavian styling: think cool geometric monochromes, simple star motifs and pops of colour. Any bold patterns are best kept to a monochrome or single-tone palette, saving vibrant rainbow hues for accent pieces, to avoid the space becoming too busy and distracting the child from sleeping. On the other hand, if ever there were a room where you could get away with theming without it appearing cheesy, it's here. Think creatively: a 'jungle safari' theme could play out with some on-trend monstera-leaf wallpaper, a (fake) animal-hide rug, a play teepee, pot plants (avoid spiky cacti, for obvious reasons) and a cute rattan bed, complete with mosquito net if you really want to go for it.

For practicality, use a hardwearing, wipe-clean paint for walls, or even add an interactive element by coating a wall in chalkboard paint, as a mini artist's space for any budding Picasso. Make sure there's a good mix of storage and display space, to hide away all the ugly plastic toys and put the pretty ones out on show. Displaying cute book covers on picture ledges can act as decor as well as encourage reading, for a double win. Keep in mind, of course, that aspiring to have a 'big girl/boy's space' can be a real selling point for little ones, so don't be afraid to steer them gently towards your way of thinking by declaring that anything truly naff is 'a bit babyish'. We won't tell.

Above: Incorporating space for a sofabed or daybed in a nursery can be wise during the early months and years. This sweet scheme incorporates dusky shades of both blue and pink, and a repurposed kitchen shelf offers useful additional wall storage.

Below left: A chalkboard wall can be great to encourage creativity. If you're concerned about living with a graffiti-scrawled room, limit it to just one wall or below the dado rail only (you could even paint it to form a graphic shape, like an abstract mountain skyline). It's possible to get colours other than black, if you prefer, and pair them with coloured chalk pens.

Below right: Vintage furniture and art prints can add real character to a child's room, and can be a charming way to incorporate special pieces from your own childhood into their sleeping space. Just make sure that any furniture you choose is sturdy and splinter-free and sand/fix/repaint it if necessary.

SQUEEZING IN SPACE: How to sneak in an extra area

How can you add more living space to a home you can't extend? Get savvy with a little repurposing in your existing space, that's how! See if one of these ideas might work for you.

1. Lean-to reading nook
Notorious for being too cold (or hot, depending on where you live), or damp and leaky, the humble lean-to is rarely viewed as anything more than storage space, but with a little spruce-up it can also provide a cosy spot for sitting, especially if it overlooks the garden. Make sure you rectify any structural problems first, then embrace its bijou proportions and fill it with cosy textures and tons of plants. Here, painting the woodwork in a Crittall-esque black gives the space a chic Scandi edge.

2. Conservatory as additional living space
By installing some form of heating (or air conditioning, if you live somewhere hot – or ideally both) and adding solar film to the roof to reduce heat and glare from the sun, you can easily transform a conservatory into a room that is usable all year round. Fill it with 'normal' household furniture rather than specific indoor/outdoor garden furniture to help the flow with the rest of your home, and use blinds or semi-sheer nets to control the light without obscuring the view.

3. Under-stairs desk
A desk tucked away under the stairs can be less intrusive than one in the main living space. Building something bespoke will make best use of awkward nooks and crannies, or you can create a more casual, DIY version with a charming vintage desk and slim shelves or pinboards on the wall above.

4. 'Shedio'
Increasingly, DIY stores are offering all-singing, all-dancing 'studio sheds' for home installation, at a fraction of the cost of a solid garden room. With myriad uses, they can offer a perfect retreat from the house for practising yoga or curling up with a good book, or even as a 'date night' dining room to escape to when the kids are tucked up in bed. Ensure yours has a power supply, and consider adding insulation to keep it toasty all year round.

5. Greenhouse workspace
This is a less obvious conversion than a shed, perhaps, but if you're not much into tomatoes, you could find that repurposing a greenhouse as a garden workspace is a fun yet practical move. Some sun protection over the roof, such as bamboo blinds or even brushwood screening (as used here), is paramount, as are roof vents (ideally ones that are controlled by a thermostat to open automatically when things get too hot) and, of course, a power supply.

1

I'm a terrible hoarder – how can I clear the clutter?

In brief: Take a systematic approach to sifting the wheat from the chaff, with the reward of a cathartic cleansing and a lovely home restyle at the end

William Morris had the right idea when he declared that we should have nothing in our homes that we do not know to be useful or believe to be beautiful. Latterly, the clutter-busting guru Marie Kondo's advice to question each object in our home and ask if it 'sparks joy', before ridding ourselves of everything that doesn't, has been so successful that to 'Kondo' one's home is now a verb. The process can be muddied for those who love being surrounded by 'stuff', but in essence both sentiments ring true, and can be a useful starting point for any decluttering exercise.

The idea of totally overhauling all your possessions can be daunting, so start small with less sentimental areas, such as kitchen cupboards or that heaving shelving unit in the corner, rather than clearing out your firstborn's nursery. Grab a timer and set yourself a (realistic) deadline to spur you on, with allocated breaks or even a schedule if you're prone to procrastination. Set up boxes or areas for different ends: recycle, bin, donate to charity, sell, keep, file and TBC. Work systematically through your chosen area, then deal with the fallout by moving everything to the spot it must now go to. Take a break, then return to your TBC pile. Do you feel able to sort this out now, or is something still holding you back? If you're still not ready, box it up separately and set yourself a date to review it again. Physical manifestations of special memories or people are precious, so consider how you could best showcase them; you could frame an early love letter between your grandparents, for example, or place baby's first bootees on a shelf. As for the rest, would making a record of it by photographing it help you to let it go?

Now you can rearrange and restyle what's left. Avoid the temptation simply to put the 'keep me' items where they were before, and instead look at things anew. Perhaps there's now space to store towels in a cupboard in the bathroom rather than on the landing, or clearing out some kitchen clutter might allow you to display crockery or tea caddies on a spare surface. You can even 'shop your house' and switch things between rooms to create a whole new look without spending a penny.

Tidy needn't mean sterile: aim for a balance of display space for the nicer stuff and hidden storage for the not-so-pretty things. Mixing in a few decorative items, like a vase of flowers or a favourite candle, will add interest and, as a bonus, a beautiful aroma.

I've spent all my money on the boring essentials and have none left for finishing touches

In brief: Seek out items that aren't strictly ornaments or artwork, for a creative, homespun look on the cheap

The process of moving house or renovating can use up all your money on the boring stuff – fees, sub-flooring and so on – leaving little in the kitty for the really fun bit, finishing things off. Remember: it's not a race. The most successful schemes often grow organically rather than being created from scratch in one sitting. That said, it is of course those trinkets and baubles that can round things off, so if your budget has been well and truly obliterated, think outside the box to create finishing touches on the cheap.

Nature is a great place to start. Forget dated dried floral arrangements and think along the lines of country-scavenger chic, displaying dried poppies, thistles or hydrangeas in winter or hedgerow- and garden-foraged flowers and foliage in summer, or even unusual feathers, shells or driftwood. Continue that thinking in your wall art, by looking for free – or bargain – alternatives. Pages cut or photocopied from a pretty book can form a striking display, and an old coffee sack – sometimes given away for free at independent coffee shops – tacked to a wall will add rustic charm; even some gorgeous gift wrap framed or fixed to the wall with washi tape is an alternative to buying a print and will cost mere small change. Vintage maps offer character and charm when used as wall art, or, if you prefer something modern, search online for downloadable artwork templates.

Add character with repurposed or recycled objects. Pretty glass drinks bottles and old food containers can be quirky pieces for odd corners, to house plant cuttings or keep small bits of clutter at bay. Tea-lights in jam jars or a simple collection of pillar candles on a table looks charmingly homespun; make them look more individual by tying ribbon or baker's twine around them. Use practical items as decor: a bar cart showcasing a handsome collection of glassware could create a talking point in a lonely corner, while freeing up cabinet space in the kitchen. If you're a crafty cat, try transforming old and unloved ornaments with a quick coat of spray paint, or re-cover a plain lampshade with a stunning offcut of fabric, for a new look in an instant.

This 'shelfie' highlights the decorative treasures that can be found on a country walk, and how hand-thrown pottery and aged terracotta can set them off to perfection. If you're keen to buy antlers to use as ornamentation and don't see any on your travels, look in gift shops situated near woodland areas or online for naturally shed (and therefore ethical) ones.

How do I know when I'm 'done'?

In brief: You'll *never* be done (sorry) ... Instead of keeping a single goal in mind, enjoy the ever-changing journey

Goals are important, of course, but the process of decorating one's home is rarely straightforward, and as soon as something seems 'complete', our needs change: a burst pipe necessitates a quick mini-renovation, or we suddenly realize that we hate our living-room curtains and won't rest until they are replaced. Try instead to embrace the process and accept that it will grow and evolve along with you, rather than being a linear path with a defined beginning and end. It can be helpful to break things down into short-, mid- and long-term goals, allowing the more pressing tasks, such as getting the plumber in to sort out that leaking tap, to take precedence over the 'someday' wistful projects, such as extending the loft.

Remember that 'done' doesn't necessarily mean perfect. There will always be something that you wish you could change. When looking at images of beautiful rooms online or in books, remember that you are seeing an edited representation of real life, leaving out the realism of that pile of ironing in the corner, or the sea of toys just out of shot. In fact, when selecting images for this book, we were careful to keep things balanced and show a selection of 'real' homes alongside places that had been professionally designed and photographed. Don't feel pressurized into changing any of your decor because of a shift in trends, either: if you still love it, embrace it (it'll come back round again sooner or later, anyway).

Changing your mindset so that you think of your space as more of a hobby, particularly if you find yourself becoming keen on interior design, can have benefits for both your home and your general well-being. Revel in the creative process of transforming that tired old coffee table into a thing of beauty, or of picking up a set of beautiful glass decanters at a vintage fair and styling them on your sideboard. Embrace an ever-growing collection of houseplants breathing life into your space, and proudly display those life-affirming mementos as you accrue them, regardless of whether they match your designated colour scheme, but simply because you love them.

Above left: Green is great for calm contemplation, especially when paired with large windows, connecting it back to nature. Here, battered painted floorboards and an imperfect old tabletop are cosied up with plush dining chairs to create a space that feels simple, yet warm and welcoming.

Above right: Bedrooms are a space where cosiness and comfort are paramount. Luxurious thick, floor-length curtains cut out unwanted light and draughts, while layering up beds with throws and cushions looks and feels lovely. Thoughtful touches – such as a handy spot to hang a favourite dressing gown, or fresh flowers by the bedside – can make all the difference.

Below: Pink has been hailed as the new neutral in recent years, as gender stereotypes continue to break down. A cool, bitter shade like this, when paired liberally with grey, cuts through notions of masculinity versus femininity and simply creates an appealing, heartfelt home, brimming with personality and soul.

Useful terms

Materials and architectural features

MDF: A versatile machined hardboard. Its perfectly flat, knotless finish makes it ideal for myriad DIY projects such as cabinetry, though it's best avoided in kitchens and bathrooms as, apart from specialist moisture-resistant MDF sheets, it doesn't cope well with moisture or liquids. It's not much of a looker, though, so it will require a paint job (use an MDF-appropriate primer first).

Plywood: Partly owing to the popularity of pale woods, plywood is increasingly being used as a wall cladding or as the material of choice for built-in furniture, offering a sleek, contemporary finish.

OSB: A cheaper, stronger alternative to plywood, Oriented Strand Board is often used as a sub-material for floors and walls. However, thanks to its interesting patina and industrial looks, it's increasingly being used for decorative applications, too.

RSJ: Commonly boxed in during construction work, lovers of a more authentic or industrial look increasingly opt to leave their Rolled Steel Joists exposed, providing a no-nonsense decorative feature. To comply with fire safety regulations, however, it must be coated with an intumescent paint (which you can finish off with a coat of standard metal paint to match your scheme).

Trims and mouldings: Details such as **architraves** (carved wooden strips used to create dado or picture rails or to frame a doorway), **cornicing** (a plaster coving blurring the line between walls and ceilings), **corbels** (ornamental brackets forming an arch shape, often used in hallways), and decorative wall panels such as plaster friezes or wooden **wainscoting** (simple raised or recessed panels covering a wall) can all add character to period and new-build properties alike. New milled wood, when painted, can be indistinguishable from old, as can lightweight polystyrene coving, or alternatively, sourcing reclaimed materials or carvings can add or replace period charm that's missing.

Popular interior styles

Scandi: An umbrella term used to describe the typically light, somewhat sparse yet still cosy homes that typify the decorating style in Nordic countries. With their cool natural light and long, dark winters, simplicity and function form the design backbone of these spaces, with pops of colour and pattern, cosy textiles such as chunky wool and fur, plus a good smattering of plants thrown in for good measure.

Rustic: Featuring mainly natural materials, often in an unfinished or (stylishly) rough state, the rustic home offers an authentic, easy space where pieces from different eras can mingle casually. Faded or even flaking paintwork can form part of the tapestry, but beware of falling into the 'shabby chic' wormhole: it can leave a space looking somewhat staged and dated.

Eclectic: Sometimes just a lazy way of describing a space containing a disparate mix of furniture and *objets*, a truly eclectic interior can perhaps be identified not just through its blending of pieces from different styles and eras (which draw influence from across the globe), but from the confidence with which it is all pulled together in an unapologetic way. Usually, in the most successful of eclectic spaces, a common design thread is evident, from a particular colour palette to a predilection for certain silhouettes.

Retro & Mid-Century: While these terms are often used interchangeably, technically Mid-Century Modern refers to pieces designed in the 1950s and '60s that follow the era's iconic geometric and elegantly tapered forms, alongside a pared-back palette that allowed its star materials – mid-toned woods such as teak and walnut, mixed with dark painted metals – to shine. Retro comes hot off its heels, adding a little more kitsch, colour and psychedelia to the mix.

'Hygge': A Danish term that has hit the design headlines hard over the past few years; it has no literal translation into English but can roughly be described as a feeling of cosy togetherness that encompasses an ethos and a way of life. This has been interpreted by designers to typify spaces that are predominantly neutral (leaning towards monochromatic greyscale) and filled with chunky throws, soft candlelight, textural accents and ubiquitous mugs of hot chocolate in front of a roaring fire.

'Lagom': Sweden's answer to *hygge*, again with no literal English translation, though it is generally interpreted to mean 'just the right amount'. In interiors it is typified by a pared-back, soft space in which ornamentation is restrained and craftsmanship revered.

Industrial: The popularity of industrial style perhaps stems partly from our desire to embrace rather than hide the fabric of our homes, and partly from its portrayal in the media as the natural habitat of city-dwelling arty hipster types. Key components of the look are exposed beams or timbers, bare brick walls and workmen's metal light fittings, all as a backdrop to an eclectic mix of found and handmade furnishings.

Minimalist: Often misinterpreted as simply meaning a pale space with not much 'stuff' in it, true minimalism is actually a hard look to really pull off, requiring a discerning eye to scrutinize the tiniest of details to ensure serene simplicity ensues. Every element, from door hinges to light switches, is designed to be fuss-free and beautiful in its own right, with clutter or excess decoration strictly frowned upon. We would say get the look by ensuring you have ample storage to keep the clutter hidden, but we suspect a true minimalist wouldn't have any clutter to begin with.

Resources

Budget bespoke

Tylko
tylko.com
Allows you to design your own bespoke shelving unit by sliding the toggle buttons to configure your perfect set-up. The price is adjusted accordingly as you tweak.

Dyke & Dean
www.dykeanddean.com
An extensive selection of industrial-inspired light fixtures, fittings, bulb holders and flexes, enabling you to design the perfect lighting configuration for any set-up.

MirrorWorld
www.mirrorworld.co.uk
Specify mirror glass by size, type, thickness, edging and fixings online, with instant quotes and fast delivery.

Superfront
www.superfront.com
A customizable range of door or drawer fronts, handles and legs designed to fit standard IKEA cabinets and popular furniture items. Their on-trend designs will transform pieces far cheaper than replacing like for like.

Vintage furniture

Flea Market Insiders
www.fleamarketinsiders.com
Great resource for finding the best flea markets around the world, searchable by country or area. Accompanying blog contains useful advice on topics such as how to ship purchases from overseas or spot genuine antiques over knock-offs.

Etsy
www.etsy.com
One of the biggest online marketplaces for vintage homewares, either in their original state or customized, redecorated and upcycled. Staff writers helpfully pull together edited stories, plus suggestions based on browsing history.

Vinterior
www.vinterior.co
Offers a discerning selection of Mid-Century, vintage and antique pieces, all carefully checked for quality and craftmanship before being added to the site.

Retrouvius
www.retrouvius.com
Sells a wide range of reclaimed doors, wooden panels and fireplaces, among other items of architectural salvage. Also offers a full interior design service for those looking for some extra help achieving the vintage look.

Specialist paints and finishes

Smarter Surfaces
www.smartersurfaces.co.uk
Offers specialist paints to turn walls into a whiteboard, chalkboard or even a magnetic surface.

Annie Sloan
www.anniesloan.com
The pioneer of chalk paint, commonly used to create an authentic aged look on furniture, plus a range of finishing waxes, stencils and books.

Frenchic
www.frenchicpaint.co.uk
Wax-infused chalk paint that simply requires a buff once dry.

Liberon
www.liberon.co.uk
Range of oils, dyes, waxes and French polishes to enhance the natural beauty of old wood.

Ronseal
www.ronseal.com
Specialist oils, primers and waxes for interior projects are available alongside their famous garden paints. The all-in-one, all-surfaces primer and undercoat can be used on many surfaces, including plastic, melamine, glass and tiles, giving a suitable sub-surface to most paints.

Earthborn
www.earthbornpaints.co.uk
Alongside their low VOC paints, they stock an acrylic-free wall glaze particularly suited to sympathetically preserving existing wall finishes in period properties.

Rustoleum (UK)
makeityours.co.uk
Extremely user-friendly site that shares project ideas and tutorials alongside links to all their products, from Chalky Finish furniture spray paint to high-shine metallic sprays.

Polycell
www.polycell.co.uk
Offers a product called Smoothover, which helps to rid walls of unflattering textured finishes that are hard to strip off, alongside a number of other clever tools and products designed to help you obtain smooth, perfect walls with minimal fuss.

Polyvine
www.polyvine.com
Sells decorator's varnish, which can be used to protect wallpaper applied to an item of furniture. Its clear matt finish will go virtually unnoticed and add longevity.

Wall decor

Juniqe
www.juniqe.co.uk
Trend-led, affordable prints with a variety of sizing and framing options.

Free Vintage Posters
www.freevintageposters.com
High-resolution image files of classic illustrated film, travel and advertising posters available to download at no cost and print yourself.

RoomFifty
www.roomfifty.com
Limited-edition prints by a regularly changing roster of 50 commercial artists, with just three prints in three sizes per artist.

Pictureframes UK
www.4x90.com
A wide selection of box, snap and certificate frames (among other styles), perfect for framing up a collection of pretty shells or a keepsake clothing item.

Decorative accents

Anthropologie
www.anthropologie.eu
Stocks an amazing selection of hardware, with jewellery-like door knobs and drawer handles to totally transform whichever surface they grace.

Secret Linen Store
www.secretlinenstore.com
Affordable yet great quality range of linen and cotton lines, with regular clearance sales to make way for new stock.

The Rug Seller
www.therugseller.co.uk
Enormous range of rugs to sift through.

Rockett St George
www.rockettstgeorge.co.uk
Full of quirky, unusual homeware and accessories featuring items you'll be unlikely to find on the high street.

Graham & Green
www.grahamandgreen.co.uk
Great for boho-influenced colourful accents.

Oliver Bonas
www.oliverbonas.com
Offers an accessible entry point for trend-led home accessories, many of which are exclusive to the brand.

Houseplants

Patch
patch.garden
An expertly curated plant range that is easy to hone down through filters so you know that you're buying plants fit for purpose. Even offers a free online video course on how to keep your houseplants alive.

Andy's Air Plants
www.andysairplants.co.uk
Set up by an air plant enthusiast to share his passion for bromeliads and *Tillandsia*, with a wide range offered both mounted and loose for use in your own displays.

Bloom
www.bloom.uk.com
A vast and surprisingly realistic selection of artificial plants and flowers in single stems and curated arrangements. Perfect for the forgetful waterer or for arrangements placed in hard-to-reach spots.

PlantSnap
www.plantsnap.com
A clever site (and accompanying app) that lets you upload images of unidentified plants – perhaps bought on impulse – and suggests what they might be, along with a description and care advice.

Children and pets

Smallable
smallable.com
Great place to build up a stylish kit of baby/kid's furniture, toys and accessories, with a cool Scandi bent.

The Modern Nursery
www.themodernnursery.com
Dedicated homewares, storage and toys for newborns upwards.

Nubie
www.nubie.co.uk
Stocks a wide range of stylish kiddie pieces, in particular some impressive baby and children's furniture lines.

Mungo & Maud
www.mungoandmaud.com
Well-made, stylish range of pet beds, bowls and household items that won't lower the tone of your interior.

Style Tails
www.styletails.com
Online magazine and shop focused on curating the world's most beautiful pet products and services.

Index

Photo credits

Front cover: Large White and Copper desk by The Hairpin Leg Co., www.thehairpinlegcompany.co.uk
Back cover: Little Greene Paint Company

4 living4media / Björnsdotter, Magdalena **7** GAP Interiors/ Douglas Gibb **9 (above left)** Loupe Images/Rachel Whiting **9 (above right)** Bureaux / Greg Cox **9 (below)** Photographer: Cathy Pyle, homeowner: Lisa Mehydene **11 (above & below)** living4media / Chiaratti, Ilaria **13 (above)** Jane Day / teawithruby.co.uk **13 (below left)** Aroundthehouses.com **13 (below right)** living4media / Möller, Cecilia **15 (above left)** living4media / Vkstockimages **15 (above right)** living4media / Chiaratti, Ilaria **15 (below)** Jeska Hearne – Lobster and Swan **17** Little Greene Paint Company **18 (#1)** Loupe Images/Rachel Whiting **18 (#2)** Tiffany Grant-Riley **19 (#3)** living4media / Scoffoni, Anne-Catherine **21 (above)** GAP Interiors/Bruce Hemming **21 (below left)** Louis Lemaire/insidehomepage **21 (below right)** living4media / Ilaria Chiaratti **23 (above left)** GAP Interiors/Julien Fernandez **23 (above right)** Styling & Photography: Klara Markbage **23 (below)** Nina Van de Goor **25** The Lovely Drawer **27 (above)** Photography: Katharine Peachey / Styling: Katy Orme **27 (below left)** GAP Interiors/ Julien Fernandez **27 (below right)** living4media / Klazinga, Jansje **29** Jen Chanyi Photography / Interior Design by Ball & Claw Vintage **31 (above left)** living4media / Möller, Cecilia **31 (above right)** Bureaux / Greg Cox **31 (below)** BOUBOUKI / Julia Bunger **32 (#1)** GAP Interiors/Bruce Hemming **32 (#2)** Photography & styling: Jolien Kadijk / Kinderkamerstylist.nl **33 (#3)** Little Greene Paint Company **35 (above)** Norsu interiors – www.norsu.com.au; styling: Jacqui Moore & Julia Green – Greenhouse Interiors; photography: Lisa Cohen **35 (below left)** Bureaux / Greg Cox **35 (below right)** Caroline Rowland / www.patchworkharmony.co.uk **37 (above left)** living4media / Chiaratti, Ilaria **37 (above right)** living4media / Jalag / Szczepaniak, Olaf **37 (below)** Tiffany Grant-Riley / 91 Magazine **39** Loupe Images/Simon Brown **41 (above)** Abi Dare / www.thesefourwallsblog.com **41 (below left)** living4media / Great Stock! **41 (below right)** living4media / View Pictures **43** Caroline Rowland / www.patchworkharmony.co.uk **45** Loupe Images/Rachel Whiting **46 (#1)** Marlous Snijder/ ohmarie.nl **47 (#2)** Bjorn Wallander / OTTO **47 (#3)** Mandi Johnson / Making Nice in the Midwest **47 (#4)** Tamsyn Morgans / www.tamsynmorgans.com **47 (#5)** Bjorn Wallander / OTTO **49** Marij Hessel /Entermyattic.com **51 (above left)** Carolyn Barber / www.timeincukcontent.com **51 (above right)** Ingvild K. Bottenvik / @ingvild90 **51 (below)** Design: Studio AC/Photography: Sarjoun Faour **53** GAP Interiors/Julien Fernandez - Architect Julie Nabucet, www.julienabucet.com **55** Belathée Photography, @belathee / design & styling of room: Jenn Elliott Blake, @jelliottblake **57** Design by Reform - www.reformcph.com / photographer: Karen Maj Kornum **59** Victoria Erdelevskaya for Heal's **60 (#1)** Liesbeth Disbergen / Sloppop Yeah **61 (#2)** living4media / Möller, Cecilia **61 (#3)** Little Greene Paint Company **61 (#4)** The Lovely Drawer **61 (#5)** Little Greene Paint Company **63 (above)** Loupe Images/Debi Treloar **63 (below left)** Loupe Images/Catherine Gratwicke **63 (below right)** GAP Interiors/Julien Fernandez **65 (above left)** living4media / Kooijman, Peter **65 (above right)** GAP Interiors/ House and Leisure **65 (below)** Betina Bianculli / @fridaflorentina **67 (above)** GAP Interiors/Bill Kingston **67 (below)** GAP Interiors/Nick Carter **69** Holly Jolliffe/Narratives/Emily Rees home **71** Heather Young / growingspaces.net **73** GAP Interiors/Dan Duchars **74 (#1)** Avenue Design Studio **75 (#2)** Loupe Images/Simon Brown **75 (#3)** living4media / Kooijman, Peter **75 (#4)** living4media / Osterlund, Rikard **75 (#5)** living4media / Wiener Wohnsinn

77 (above) GAP Interiors/Jake Fitzjones - Architect - Martins Camisuli Architects and Designers; Stylist - Shani Zion **77 (below left)** GAP Interiors/Dan Duchars **77 (below right)** living4media / Klazinga, Jansje **79 (above left)** GAP Interiors/ Nick Smith - Hannah Brown and Lucy Heathcoat of Amory Brown **79 (above right)** living4media / Pics On-Line / Tuesday, June **79 (below)** living4media / Wojnar, Radoslaw **81 (above & below)** Fran Parente/OTTO **83 (above)** living4media /Chiaratti, Ilaria **83 (below left)** living4media / Struve, Nina **83 (below right)** Tiffany Grant-Riley **85** Allison Sadler / www.allissonsadler. co.uk **87 (above)** GAP Interiors/David Cleveland **87 (below)** living4media / Klazinga, Jansje **88 (#1, left)** Interior design & photography: Sarah Akwisombe **88 (#1, right)** GAP Interiors/ Julien Fernandez **89 (#2)** Photographer: Cathy Pyle, homeowner: Lisa Mehydene **89 (#3)** Jemma Watts / 91 Magazine **89 (#4, top)** Interior design & photography: Sarah Akwisombe **89 (#4, bottom)** west elm Mobile Chandelier – Large in Antique Bronze; west elm, www.westelm.co.uk **89 (#5, top)** Kimberly Duran / www.swoonworthy.co.uk **89 (#5, bottom)** living4media / Hogan, Sarah **91 (above left)** GAP Interiors/Julien Fernandez **91 (above right)** GAP Interiors/Julien Fernandez – Ninou Etienne ñ Fusion D Agency – www.fusiond.fr **91 (below)** living4media / Scoffoni, Anne-Catherine **93 (above)** Photographer: Cathy Pyle, homeowner: Lisa Mehydene **93 (below left)** Caroline Rowland / www.patchworkharmony.co.uk **93 (below right)** living4media / Möller, Cecilia **95 (above left)** living4media / Simon Maxwell Photography **95 (above right)** living4media / Hessel, Marij **95 (below)** living4media / Joosten, Pauline **97** Jemma Watts **99 (above)** Carole Poirot / Prop Stylist & Photographer - carolepoirot.com **99 (below left & right)** Bureaux / Greg Cox **101** GAP Interiors/Rachael Smith and Victoria Tunstall **102 (#1)** Fired Earth -Geometric (paint colours: Yes Your Honour, Storm, Orchard Pink, Graphite and Skyline Grey) **103 (#2)** Linda Dekkers / Live Loud Girl / www.liveloudgirl. com **103 (#3)** GAP Interiors/Sandra van Aalst **103 (#4)** GAP Interiors/Bruce Hemming - www.folkathomestore.com **103 (#5)** Paint and Paper Library **105 (above left)** Bureaux / Greg Cox **105 (above right)** Living 4 Media **105 (below)** Jemma Watts **107 (above)** Photography: Katharine Peachey / Styling: Katy Orme **107 (below left)** Oliver Gordon **107 (below right)** GAP Interiors/Julien Fernandez **109 (above left)** Kimberly Duran / www.swoonworthy.co.uk **109 (above right)** Marlous Snijder/ ohmarie.nl **109 (below)** Photographer: Cathy Pyle, homeowner: Lisa Mehydene **111** Tamsyn Morgans / www. tamsynmorgans.com **113** GAP Interiors/Julien Fernandez **115** living4media / Chiaratti, Ilaria **116 (#1)** Bureaux / Greg Cox **117 (#2)** Avenue Design Studio **117 (#3)** 'A Vase of Flowers with Berries and Insects': mural from the Ashmolean Collection at surfaceview.co.uk **117 (#4)** Tiffany Grant-Riley **117 (#5)** living4media /Vkstockimages **119 (above)** At Home in Love **119 (below left)** Loupe Images/Simon Brown **119 (below right)** Kasia Fiszer **121** Matilda Hildingsson / Babes in Boyland **123** Photography & Styling: Cate St Hill **125 (above left)** Laura Gummerman via abeautifulmess.com **125 (above right)** Dee Campling **125 (below)** Graham Atkins-Hughes/TIA Digital Ltd **127** Loupe Images/Catherine Gratwicke **129 (above)** Katy Orme / Apartment Apothecary blog **129 (below left)** GAP Interiors/Julien Fernandez **129 (below right)** Elise Grossman **130 (#1)** Tiffany Grant-Riley **131 (#2)** GAP Interiors/ Rachel Whiting **131 (#3)** GAP Interiors/House and Leisure - Photographs and Styling: Micky Hoyle **131 (#4)** Jeska Hearne - Lobster and Swan **131 (#5)** Maria Bell Photography **133** GAP Interiors/David Cleveland **135** Kym Grimshaw **137 (above left)** Avenue Design Studio **137 (above right)** Katy Orme / Apartment Apothecary blog **137 (below)** living4media / Möller, Cecilia

The author would like to thank:

Thanks to all the creative photographers, designers, bloggers and image-makers who gave us permission to illustrate these pages with their work.

A heartfelt thank you to Liz Faber for originally approaching me with this book concept, and for trusting me to flesh it out and steer things forward in my own direction. Latterly, thanks to Felicity Maunder for her dedicated direction once the project got fully underway, and to Caroline Rowland for her brilliant picture-sourcing skills – no mean feat at times given my somewhat exacting standards! Thanks to Rosie Fairhead for respectfully editing my words while still retaining my tone of voice, and to Masumi Briozzo for transforming it all into the book you hold in your hands today.

Personally, I'd like to thank the many friends and family members I badgered into sharing their interior design dilemmas with me in order to help me pull together what has hopefully been some useful questions shared by many of you. As always, a thank you to my Dad for being my unofficial/unpaid DIY and Electricals Technical Consultant, and to my Mum for the myriad sewing questions often thrown her way. And to my own little family: my partner, Paul, always my number one supporter, and our little rescue dog, Stella, for keeping me company and acting as my (albeit not very effective) sounding board as I wrote. And to you, the reader: I truly hope this book has answered all your existing dilemmas, along with many others you never even knew you had.

LAURENCE KING

Published in 2019 by
Laurence King Publishing
361-373 City Road,
London EC1V 1LR,
United Kingdom
enquiries@laurenceking.com
www.laurenceking.com

Reprinted 2019

© Text 2019 Joanna Thornhill

Joanna Thornhill has asserted her right under the Copyright, Designs, and Patents Act 1988 to be identified as the Author of this Work.

A catalogue record for this book is available from the British Library.

ISBN: 978 1 78627 386 4

Design: Masumi Briozzo
Picture research: Caroline Rowland
Senior editor: Felicity Maunderww

Printed in China

Laurence King Publishing is committed to ethical and sustainable production. We are proud participants in The Book Chain Project ®
bookchainproject.com